Fostering A Sense of Wonder During the Early Childhood Years

Ruth A. Wilson, Ph.D.

Copyright © 1993 by Ruth A. Wilson. All rights reserved. Printed in the United States of America. Except as permitted under the United States Copyright Act of 1976, no part of this publication may be reproduced or distributed in any form or by any means, or stored in a data base retrieval system, without prior written permission of Ruth A. Wilson.

ISBN 1-57074-045-3
Printer/Binder: Greyden Press

Dedication

To all teachers of young children in recognition of the important role you play in their lives today and in the future. Know that the experiences you provide make a lasting difference not only for individual children but for the world as well.

ACKNOWLEDGMENTS

A wonderful group of people participated in the development of this book. Most directly were three graduate assistants who took a personal interest in the project and gave generously of their time, talents, and energy. These individuals are Melinda Geithmann, Jann Frisk, and Jodie Smith. To each of you, I say thank you and want you to know that you've been a joy to work with. I also wish to thank the Center for Environmental Programs at Bowling Green State University and the team of people there; Thomas (Berry) Cobb, Justine Magsig, and Eleanor Connor. You, too, have been wonderful partners in the Environmental Education for Preschoolers project. Other special people are Steve and Deb McKee, Michelle Lach, the members of the community advisory committee, professional review team, and the teachers at Toledo Day Nursery. Thank you for your support and suggestions.

Photos and artwork are from Toledo Day Nursery in Toledo, Ohio and the Child Development Center at Bowling Green State University.

This project was funded, in part, by the Ohio Environmental Education Fund (OEEF), an office of the Ohio Environmental Protection Agency, Columbus, Ohio through a grant to Bowling Green State University, Bowling Green, Ohio and directed by Dr. Ruth A. Wilson. The second printing of this document is made possible by the OEEF for free distribution. Additional copies may be obtained from the OEEF by writing to P.O. Box 1049, Columbus, Ohio 43216-1049 or by calling (614) 644-2873.

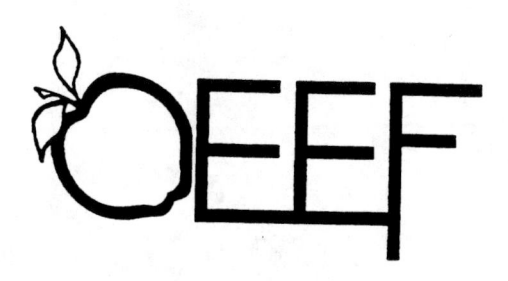

Ruth Wilson

Dr. Ruth Wilson's work of the past several years has focused on a merging of environmental education and early childhood education and has included the development of a curriculum guide (Fostering a Sense of Wonder During the Early Childhood Years) the establishment of an international network and resource center, the publication and dissemination of the "Earthworm" newsletter, the development of a monograph (Environmental Education at the Early Childhood Level), and the publication of numerous articles in professional journals. Dr. Wilson leads teacher training workshops in early childhood environmental education, is a frequent presenter at state and national conferences, and has served as a consultant to the development and enhancement of early childhood environmental education programs in a variety of settings (e.g., nature centers, zoos, preschools, family home day care providers, etc.). Dr. Wilson is currently involved in research on how to make outdoor play spaces for young children more nature-oriented, how to identify and describe young children's way of knowing and experiencing the natural world, and how to use environmental autobiographies as a vehicle for understanding and enhancing one's relationship to the natural environment. For further information, contact

Dr. Ruth Wilson
Department of Special Education
Bowling Green State University
Bowling Green, OH 43403
419/372-7278 (W) or 419-474-0871 (H)
FAX: 419/372-8265
E-Mail: rwilso2@andy.bgsu.edu

Table of Contents

Dedication	iii
Acknowledgments	v
Table of Contents	vii
List of Activities	viii
Implementation Guidelines	ix
Preface	xi

Part I: For Children and the Earth 1
   Chapter 1   Science and Beyond 3
   Chapter 2   Integrating Environmental Education and
                      Early Childhood Education 9
   Chapter 3   Guidelines and Suggestions for
                      Fostering a Sense of Wonder 13

Part II: Implementing the Curriculum 25
   Chapter 4   Indoor Discoveries 27
      Learning Centers: Bringing the Outdoors In 27
      Animals and Plants in the Classroom 31
      Books and Stories 39
      Fun With Art: Encouraging Expressions of Wonder 47
      Music and Movement 59
      Enjoying the Seasons 67
      Learning About Food 87
      Group Activities 101
      Enriching the Classroom Environment 109
   Chapter 5   Outdoor Excursions 113
     Field Trips
     Enjoying Nature in Your Own Backyard 131

Part III: Special Considerations 141
   Chapter 6   Individualizing the Program 143
      Special Needs and Interests 143
      Involving Families 149
   Chapter 7   Enhancing Your Appreciation of Nature 151

Part IV: Evaluating Your Program 155
   Chapter 8   Fostering a Love of Nature Index 157

Final Thoughts	173
References	175
Index	177
Appendices	181
Biological Supply Companies	183
Pro-Nature Children's Books	185
Themes and Books	189
Resources for Teachers (Annotated Bibliography)	193

List of Activities

Activity	Page
Adopt An Animal	124
Animal Prints	53
Animal Tracks	105
Artistic Arrangements	57
Beauty on the Ground and All Around	48
Capture Real Snowflakes	75
Celebrate the Coming of Spring	82
Cracking A Coconut	99
Collect Animal Tracks	130
Discovering How Plants Drink	93
Dressing a Tree	85
Enjoying Raw Vegetables	90
Enjoying Rice	97
Enjoying the Harvest	69
Enjoying the Seasons	67
Fascinating Shapes	49
Finding Seeds in Food	91
Finding the New Plant in an Onion Bulb	92
Fruit and Vegetable Prints	52
Fun in the Snow	73
Grow Your Own Icicle	72
Growing Flowers	80
Growing Food Plants	88
Halloween Fun	68
The Hiding Game	106
Homemade Peanut Butter	95
Imitate Animals	65
Introducing an Animal to the Children	145
Learning That Plants are Wildlife, Too	125
Listen to Music About Nature	62
Making Christmas/Winter Decorations	71
Making Flour	94
Mobiles	54
Multisensory Springtime Walk	77
Natural Straws	83
Nature Boxes	58
Nature Charades	66
Nature's Musical Instruments	64
Painting With Nature's Colors	56
Paper Snowflakes	74
Popping Popcorn	98
Real and Pretend Photos	55
Rubbings From Trees and Other Things	50
The Sharing Circle: Learning to Show Respect	103
Sound Recordings From Nature	60
Sprout Plants Indoors	76
Sprouting Beans	79
Start a Compost Pile	136
Taking Pictures Over Time	84
A Terrarium for the Classroom	110
Toasting Pumpkin Seeds	96
Wildlife Hunt	122
Window Hangings	51

Implementation Guidelines

1. Introduce nature-related materials and activities in the different learning centers. .... Page 27-30
2. Make animals and plants a part of the classroom environment. .... Page 31-37
3. Share pro-nature books with children. .... Page 39-45
4. Encourage nature-related art activities. .... Page 47-58
5. Introduce nature-related music and movement activities. .... Page 59-66
6. Celebrate each of the seasons with special nature-related activities. .... Page 67-86
7. Demonstrate the connection between the food we eat and the world of nature. .... Page 87-100
8. Introduce a variety of nature-related themes and concepts through group activities. .... Page 101-107
9. Display nature-related art and use materials from the natural world to decorate the classroom. .... Page 109-111
10. Go on a variety of nature-study field trips. .... Page 113-130
11. Introduce children to wildlife and other aspects of nature in and around the school yard. .... Page 131-139
12. Individualize the program to meet special needs and interests. .... Page 143-148
13. Invite parent participation in nature-related activities. .... Page 149-150
14. Enhance your own understanding and appreciation of the natural world. .... Page 151-153

"In the end we will conserve only what we love."

Lao-Tsu

Preface

This book is based on the understanding that fostering a sense of wonder and appreciation for the natural world is important to the development of young children and the preservation of Planet Earth. It is written in a spirit of caring deeply about the natural world and the quality of life we pass on to our children. It is also written in a spirit of caring for young children and the types of experiences they have during their early childhood years. This book is based on the belief that fostering a love of nature will add immensely to the aesthetic development of young children and will give them a gift which can make their lives more meaningful and joyful throughout both childhood and adult life. It is also based on the belief that experiences children have early in life impact on the attitudes and behaviors they carry with them throughout their lifetime.

In a society as we know it today, children do not automatically develop an awareness and appreciation of the natural world. There are, in fact, many forces which tend to foster a prejudice against nature rather than an appreciation for it. We've adopted "greenhouse" ways of living, where 95% of our time is spent indoors. We use temperature and climate control systems in our homes, cars, and places of business. Children travel to school in buses or cars and then sit in classes surrounded by walls of concrete and steel. For recreation and relaxation, they turn to movie theaters, restaurants, malls, and video arcades. Is it any wonder, then, that so many children grow up without a sense of connectedness with the natural world? How can children learn an appreciation for the wonder and mystery of nature when their very way of life shields them from intimate contacts with the natural world?

Rachel Carson, in her book, *The Sense of Wonder*, speaks of an "inborn sense of wonder," but indicates that if a child is to keep this magic alive, he or she "needs the companionship of at least one adult who can share it, rediscovering with him the joy, excitement and mystery of the world we live in." And that, precisely, is what this book is all about—that is, ideas on how to be that "special adult" who can foster a sense of wonder in young children.

This book is divided into four major sections. The first section outlines some ideas on what an early childhood environmental education program encompasses—addressing both what a quality environmental education program for preschoolers is and what it is not. Critical to this point is the understanding that an environmental education program is not the same as a science program. There are certain concepts, attitudes, and behaviors that are unique to an environmental education program which may or may not be included in a science program. Environmental education, as outlined by the approach in this book, emphasizes the affective and aesthetic development of the young child versus a concentration on cognitive development, as a science curriculum is more likely to do.

The first part of the book also examines the appropriateness of environmental education at the early childhood level. Parallels are drawn between what is known about "developmentally appropriate practices" in early childhood education (Bredekamp, 1987) and the basic understandings about what constitutes a quality environmental education program. Overlapping characteristics between environmental education and early childhood education suggest that the integration of these two disciplines is both feasible and desirable.

In addition to providing a theoretical basis for integrating environmental education and early childhood education, the first section of this book also offers practical guidelines and suggestions for developing an early childhood environmental education program. In this section, the role of the adult is discussed, as are ideas on how to keep children interested and actively involved. Finally, specific goals and objectives for an early childhood environmental education program are also presented.

The second part of the book is devoted to practical ideas on how to infuse environmental education into all aspects of the early childhood curriculum. This section includes ideas on how to use learning centers for fostering an understanding and appreciation of the natural world, how to choose pro-nature children's literature, how to incorporate environmental education into music, art, and group activities, and how to enrich the classroom environment with objects from nature. This section also includes ideas on what to do outdoors to foster an appreciation of nature—what kinds of field trips to take, what to do on nature walks, how to enhance the school yard, and how to tap into community resources.

Part three of the books addresses "special considerations" in developing and implementing an early childhood environmental education program. Topics addressed in this section include dealing with fears, working with children with disabilities, working with infants and toddlers, and involving families. Also included in this section is a discussion on what teachers can do to enhance their own understanding and appreciation of nature.

The fourth part of the book deals with program evaluation and offers a self-rating scale that can be used as a tool for evaluating and enhancing one's own early childhood environmental education program. Items on the scale coincide with the implementation guidelines presented throughout the book.

An Appendix to the book offers several annotated bibliographies of related resources. One bibliography outlines resource materials for the teacher; a second bibliography presents books for children.

Fostering a Sense of Wonder During the Early Childhood Years, then, addresses theory, practical applications, and information on appropriate resources—all designed to help early childhood educators foster a sense of wonder about the natural world.

Part I

For Children and the Earth

*"This curious world which we inhabit is more wonderful
than it is convenient; more beautiful than it is useful;
it is more to be admired and enjoyed than used."*

Henry David Thoreau

"Sensitiveness to life is the highest product of education."
Liberty Hyde Bailey

Chapter 1
Science and Beyond*

Science Education

Science, as an area of study, is usually defined in terms of knowledge. It deals with facts and laws arranged in an orderly system. Science means "to know" and is usually thought of in relation to rational knowledge. Science can also be defined in terms of an approach, or technique, for learning about the natural world, and includes such skills as observation, description, problem solving, classification, comparison, verifying, hypothesizing, seeing relationships, and inferring.

Because science includes a study of the natural world, many people tend to equate environmental education with science education. This belief, however, does not do justice to what environmental education can do for children and the Earth. Environmental education should be more than a part of the science education program and should include experiences and goals that typically go beyond the boundaries of science.

---

*Note: An earlier version of this section was originally published in *INFO*, a newsletter of the West Central Ohio Regional Resource Center, Spring, 1992.

Environmental Education

While science and the development of rational thinking are important during the preschool years, early experiences with nature should not focus exclusively—or even primarily—on facts to be learned and scientific methods of investigation to be followed. Environmental education, especially at the early childhood level, needs to be broader than science and should focus more on affect and intuitive knowledge than on facts and rational knowledge. An environmental education program should foster sensitivity to the beauty of nature and an attitude of caring about what happens to our natural environment. The emphasis should be on the development of caring and a personal relationship toward other living things. The program should also foster respect for the interrelationships that exist among all aspects of the natural environment.

An environmental education program for young children should serve as the first step in the development of an environmentally literate and concerned citizenry. It should cultivate "a right way of thinking and acting" (Trant, 1986, p. 23). But, facts alone aren't enough to change people's relationship to nature. A look at conservation programs focusing only on informing the public of threats to the natural environment indicate that this approach is not successful. If our environmental problems are to be solved, attitudes too must change (Trant, 1986).

Environmental education should be thought of as a process, rather than a field of study to be mastered. It should be a process of developing, not only knowledge and skills, but also awareness, values, attitudes, and sensitivities. It should be "a process of learning to make decisions and acquiring a code of behavior about ethical and qualitative issues" (Trant, 1986, p. 18). An environmental education program should foster a sense of appreciation and caring. It should develop in young children attitudes of stewardship, safe-keeping, and responsibility.

While environmental education is critically important for the preservation of the natural environment, it is also important for the development of the whole child. Environmental education programs can contribute to a sense of self and personal competence. It can nurture one's sense of wonder and contribute to a "necessary humility"—which, as discussed by Rachel Carson (1956) in *The Sense of Wonder*—is important for quality of life and for perspective on the human relationship to nature. While the study of science emphasizes intellectual growth, environmental education invites the child to experience a sense of his or her wholeness, as an integrated physical, mental, emotional and spiritual being (Miles, 1986-87).

The immediacy of the natural environment involves focusing awareness on the here and now and helps young children become more aware of their environment, which includes the self (Miles, 1986-87). This awareness can help children understand how humans *are nature* and may result in "a greater respect for life and appreciation for other life forms and even other persons" (Miles, 1986-87, p. 37). Environmental education, then, fosters a sense of connectedness and an appreciation of this connectedness. Environmental education with young children should also stimulate their curiosity and interest in the world around them. It should teach them to observe the phenomena of nature and kindle a desire to learn more about the wonders and complexities of the natural world. As most early childhood educators realize, such a desire is fostered by opportunities to explore and discover, not by being taught facts about nature. In his book *Emile,* Jean Jacques Rosseau pointed the way : "Teach your child to observe the phenomena of nature. . . . Let him know nothing because you have told him but because he has learnt it himself. Let him not be taught science, let him discover it. . . . begin by showing him the real thing so that he may at least know what you are talking about."

Environmental education is also about experiencing the beautiful and helping children discover "the poetical, the mystical, the imaginative and creative side of the human being" (Trant, 1986, p. 23). This aspect of human development has traditionally been neglected, not only in scientific programs, but in general education programs, as well. "Schooling today is perhaps over-intellectual. It has become too abstract and too cognitive" (Trant, 1986, p. 22).

The dangers of an over-intellectual approach are especially acute at the early childhood level. Early childhood educators have long recognized the dangers of an "academic approach" to preschool education, even to the point of labeling such an approach "miseducation" (Elkind, 1988). We do, indeed, want young children to know about nature, but such knowing must include awareness, intuition, and inspiration.

A Comparison of Goals

Environmental education goals. Goals of an environmental education program for young children should include (a) the development of a sense of wonder, (b) an appreciation for the beauty and mystery of the natural world, (c) opportunities to experience the joy of closeness to nature, and (d) respect for other creatures. Rather than being in conflict with the goals of a science education program, these goals tend to extend and enhance what science has to offer.

Science education goals. Science programs for young children often include the following four goals: (a) the development of problem-solving skills; (b) the development of a scientific attitude; (c) the gaining of scientific knowledge and information; and (d) the development of interest and appreciation in science all around us. While these goals may seem, at first, to differ considerably from the goals outlined above for a nature education program, overlap between the two is not difficult to illustrate. One place to start is with a discussion of how the world of nature can be used as a means of achieving the science goals.

Combining the goals. The first science goal listed above is the development of problem-solving skills and can be easily combined with several environmental education goals. Teachers can foster the development of problem-solving skills by tapping into the natural curiosity of children and by encouraging them to be good observers. Children are naturally curious about the natural world and have in the world around them unlimited opportunities for exploration and experimentation. Teachers can take children's questions about the natural world and present them back to the children as problems to be solved. The question of "Why did the snow go away?" can be handed back to the child with an invitation to do some problem solving on his or her own. "Maybe we can find out," is an excellent lead-in to further investigations.

Frequent changes in the world of nature invite questioning and problem solving. Such changes also encourage frequent and careful observations. Observing, questioning, and problem solving tend to foster a sense of wonder and an appreciation for the mystery of the natural world while, at the same time, meeting several objectives of a science education program.

The development of a scientific attitude is a science goal that involves, among other things, careful observations, measurements, classifications, predictions, and inferences. Many of these processes are the same ones young children spontaneously use when they interact with the natural world, discovering attributes, organizing schema, and representing the world. At the early childhood level, experiences in science can include opportunities for young children to learn some of the processes of science as they observe and describe attributes and actions. Concepts about animals, plants, weather, water, and stones are all appropriate for young children to investigate as they grow in the development of a scientific attitude.

The development of a scientific attitude is dependent, to a great extent, on access to materials that help children understand objects and their actions and interactions. The benefits of access to materials in nature, however, extend beyond the intellectual concepts developed as a result of interacting with such materials. Access to nature also fosters the development of a sense of wonder, an appreciation for the beauty and mystery of the natural world, and opportunities to experience the joy of closeness to nature—all important aspects of an environmental education program.

Helping children gain scientific knowledge and information is the third goal of science education. An immediate source of knowledge—and one that is most appropriate for young children—is the natural world, itself. Young children learn by acting on the world around them. Thus, they need access to concrete materials—materials that are real and which they can manipulate. For young children, knowledge is constructed through their interactions with materials. They come to know an object by acting on it. They learn from the data they take in through their senses and from what happens when they physically manipulate an object. Thus, the source of scientific knowledge and information for young children is through direct experience, not text books, films, or lectures.

Fortunately, the world of nature offers unlimited opportunities for children to learn through direct, sensorimotor experiences. The sights, smells, textures, and sounds of nature all invite hands-on exploration and experimentation. Thus, content and motivation for gaining scientific knowledge and information are easily accessible through the world of nature.

The fourth science goal has to do with the development of interest and appreciation in science all around us and meshes extremely well with the desired outcomes of an environmental education program. Because nature can be found everywhere and invites active engagement on the part of young children, it can serve as the primary vehicle for fostering interest and appreciation in science. Moss on the side of a tree, vegetables growing in a garden, and birds hovering around a feeder—all tend to elicit a great deal of curiosity and wonder. What better place to spark an interest in science than through the world of nature!

Conclusions and Implications

Environmental education offers a way of knowing that includes, but is not limited to, rational knowledge. Its focus is on a way of knowing that moves the heart and soul and imagination of the one involved. For the young child, this way of knowing can add more to quality of life than any amount of rational knowledge can ever give. It can serve as "an unfailing antidote against the boredom and disenchantments of later years, the sterile preoccupation with things that are artificial, the alienation from the sources of our strength" (Carson, 1956, p. 43).

Environmental education at the early childhood level is more about *feeling* than *knowing*. It's about arousing "a sense of the beautiful, the excitement of the new and the unknown, a feeling of sympathy, pity, admiration or love" (Carson, 1956, p. 45). Environmental education can serve as a catalyst in fostering the affective and aesthetic development of the young child.

While it is, indeed, good to have factual information about the natural world, it is also important to have a sense of connectedness, love, and caring for the world of nature. It is through this "other way of knowing" that children come to a better understanding of who they are in relation to their environment. They come to know that they are part of—not separate from—the natural world. The benefits of such a realization will not only enrich the lives of young children, but will help to ensure the well-being of Earth as well.

Recommended Resources

Early Childhood and Science. M. McIntyre. Washington, D.C.: National Science Teacher's Association, 1984.

The Sense of Wonder. R. Carson. New York: Harper & Row, 1965

"Now I see the secret of the making of the best person. It is to grow in the open air, and to eat and sleep with the earth."

Walt Whitman

Chapter 2
Integrating Environmental Education and Early Childhood Education

Rationale

Environmental education and early childhood education are two different areas of education, each having its own philosophy, goals, and instructional materials; yet, the two have much in common. In early childhood education, "best practices" are outlined by "developmentally appropriate practices," and call for active exploration, problem solving activities, and social interaction (Bredekamp, 1987). These "best practices" match well the "key characteristics" of environmental education, which include (1) active, rather than passive, learning opportunities; (2) direct, rather than abstract, experiences with nature and natural systems; and (3) free exploration on the part of the students (Cohen, 1992).

Both early childhood education and environmental education are built on an understanding of how children learn—that is, by interacting with the natural environment. Children construct an understanding of their world by acting upon the natural environment around them—primarily through their senses and motoric manipulation.

Because children learn by exploring and experimenting, they are excellent candidates for field study experiences. They enjoy and learn from direct experiences with nature through such activities as nature walks oriented around sensory experiences (touching, smelling, hearing, seeing, etc.).

Early childhood education uses a child-centered, versus teacher-directed, approach. Early childhood educators realize that young children learn best in an atmosphere that allows freedom of choice and movement, spontaneous initiation of activities, and informal conversations. Thus, they try to create a classroom environment that is open and non-directive (Widerstrom, 1986). Teachers in a child-centered program focus on the child's interests and capitalize on the "teachable moments" that occur frequently throughout the day.

A child-centered approach is ideal for learning about the natural world. Children do not need direct instruction on how to feel, see, and hear the world around them. Nor is there just one right way to experiment with stones, sticks, and water. Children learn best from their early investigations and experiments in the out-of-doors—or with materials gathered from the out-of-doors—when their activities are guided by interest and curiosity, not by prescribed methods of inquiry.

The focus of early childhood education is on the development of the whole child, versus being limited to the cognitive or academic domain. With this focus, environmental education has invaluable resources to offer. Experiences with the natural world tend to be rich in opportunities for fostering growth in all the developmental domains, including the adaptive, aesthetic, cognitive, communication, sensorimotor, and social-emotional.

Environmental education can help young children not only discover the world around them, but help them better understand themselves as well. As young children grow in an understanding of the natural world, they soon discover that they are a part of nature. Through varied experiences with the natural world, they begin to develop a sense of wholeness and connectedness with all living things.

Appropriate Goals and Objectives

An early childhood environmental education program requires more than a set of nature-related activities. Also required is some type of framework or structure to give it consistency and continuity. The following set of goals and related understandings might be used to structure a developmentally appropriate environmental education program for young children. It is around this framework that the curriculum guide, *Fostering a Sense of Wonder During the Early Childhood Years,* has been written.

Goal 1: To develop an awareness and enjoyment of the beauty and wonder of the natural world.
   Related Understandings:
   - The natural world is full of beauty and wonder.
   - Many works in art, music, and literature are based on different aspects of nature.
   - The natural world can be a source of personal joy and inspiration.

Goal 2: To become aware of the concepts of cycles, diversity, and interconnectedness in nature
   Related Understandings:
   - The natural world is in a state of constant change.
   - Everything in nature is connected.
   - All living things, including people, need food, air and water to survive.
   - All the resources we use come from the natural world.
   - Wildlife is found everywhere.
   - Diversity is a part of the natural environment.

Goal 3: To develop a sense of appreciation and respect for the integrity of the natural world
   Related Understandings:
   - The natural world is ordered, balanced, and harmonious.
   - Change is a natural part of the workings of the earth.
   - All living and non-living things should be treated with respect.

Goal 4: To develop a sense of caring for Planet Earth and an understanding of how different types of pollution might harm the Earth
   Related Understandings:
   - Earth is our home.
   - We need to relate to the natural environment in a respectful, caring way.

- There are many different types of pollution—noise pollution, visual pollution, air pollution, water pollution, etc.
- Pollution tends to destroy the natural environment and our enjoyment of it.

Goal 5: To develop an awareness that people are a part of the natural world, not separate from it
  Related Understandings:
  - The health and well being of people are effected by the quality of the natural environment.
  - The actions of individuals and groups effect other individuals, society, and the natural environment.

Goal 6: To develop an understanding of how to contribute to the well-being of the Earth
  Related Understandings:
  - We can reduce pollution by picking up trash.
  - We can help save the Earth by recycling.
  - We should respect and take care of all aspects of the natural world.
  - We should live lightly on the Earth.

Recommended Resources

Science Experiences for the Early Childhood Years. J. Harlan. New York: Merril Publishing, 1988.

Bridging Early Childhood and Nature Education. Jamestown, NY: Roger Tory Peterson Institute, 1991.

Discover the World: Empowering Children to Value Themselves, Others and the Earth. S. Hopkins & J. Winters, Philadelphia, PA: New Society Publishers, 1990.

Keepers of the Animals: Native American Stories and Wildlife Activities for Children. M. Caduto & J. Bruchac. Golden, CO: Fulcrum Publishing, 1991.

Keepers of the Animals: Teacher's Guide. M. Caduto & J Bruchac. Golden, CO: Fulcrum Publishing, 1992.

Keepers of the Earth: Native American Stories and Environmental Activities for Children. M. Caduto & J. Bruchac. Golden, CA: Fulcrum, Inc. 1989.

Acclimatization. S. Van Matre. Martinsville, IN: American Camping Association, 1972.

"It is not half so important to know as to feel."
Rachel Carson

Chapter 3
Guidelines and Suggestions for Fostering a Sense of Wonder

Basic Guidelines

A sense of wonder cannot be taught. It can only come by way of insight and discovery. Early childhood educators are aware of this, as are teachers in environmental education programs. They recognize that the path to a sense of wonder regarding the natural world is through a variety of positive personal experiences with the world of nature.

Based on the understanding of how young children learn and what is considered best practices in both early childhood education and environmental education, the following list of guidelines have been developed for implementing an environmental education program for preschoolers. Following this listing, is a discussion of each of these items.

- Begin with simple experiences.
- Keep children actively involved.
- Provide pleasant, memorable experiences.
- Emphasize experiencing versus teaching.
- Involve full use of the senses.
- Provide multimodal learning experiences.
- Focus on relationships.
- Demonstrate a personal interest in and enjoyment of the natural world.
- Model caring for the natural environment.
- Maintain a warm, accepting, and nurturing atmosphere.
- Introduce multicultural experiences and perspectives.
- Focus on the beauty and wonder of nature.
- Go outside whenever possible.
- Infuse environmental education into all aspects of the early childhood program.

Begin with simple experinces. "Overloading" is a dangerous practice in many fields of endeavor, including education and education about the natural world. In introducing young children to the world of nature, the best place to start is with the most immediate environment. Children need to feel comfortable and unafraid; they need to know that the natural world is a safe place to be.

Many young children come to school with little or no direct experience with natural environments. They may, thus, have little understandings and great fears about what may happen to them in their encounters with nature. They may fear the darkness of a wooded area. They may think that all bugs and insects bite or sting. In their minds, an earthworm may be a poisonous snake. Such children need a gradual exposure to the world of nature. They need to become familiar with the trees and bushes in the school yard before they'll feel comfortable hiking in the woods. They'll have to observe and care for classroom pets before they're asked to welcome a caterpillar crawling across their hand or feel the wooly head of a lamb while on a field trip to a farm.

Young children also need to realize that nature is all around them and that wildlife can be found anywhere. Some children seem to think that wildlife is somehow very separate and far away from where they live. When asked where he might look to find wildlife, one child responded by saying, "Africa!" For such children, one of the most meaningful lessons would focus on becoming aware of wildlife in their immediate environment.

Ideas on how to begin with simple experiences include:
- watching a bean seed sprout in the classroom before attempting the planting and tending of a vegetable garden
- playing with snow in the texture table before making and crawling through tunnels of snow in the school yard
- watching birds and squirrels from a "window on nature" before suggesting that a pony eat from their hands
- walking barefoot in the grass and sand before wading in a shallow stream.

Keep children actively involed.
Young children learn most effectively when they are engaged in interactions, rather than in merely receptive or passive activities (Katz, 1987). Children's interactions should be with adults, materials and their surroundings (Bredekamp, 1987).

To keep children actively involved, teachers must serve as facilitators, enablers and consultants ((Harlan, 1992). As facilitators, teachers create a learning environment that will be inviting and responsive. Such an environment may be one in which children are allowed to be messy and get messy. It invites exploration and experimentation and lets the children know that they are competent.

As enablers, teachers help children become aware of themselves as thinkers and problem-solvers (Harlan, 1992). Rather than serving as the ultimate source of knowledge, teachers help children realize that they can discover (or construct) their own knowledge. Enablers share the excitement of discovery with the children and value the process of experimenting and exploring as much as (or more than!) the outcome.

As consultants, teachers observe carefully, listen closely, and answer questions simply (Harlan, 1992). The teacher supports rather than directs the child's learning. It is the child's interest, curiosity, and need to know that set the agenda and drive the activity. While the teacher may introduce the idea of "looking for signs of spring" during a nature walk, children's unanticipated interest in pebbles along a stream or leaves decaying under a log will be attended to and supported. Far better to foster a sense of wonder through what the children find of interest than to adopt an "instructor's mode" and try to teach facts about what the teacher feels to be important for the children to know.

At the early childhood level, the most important "facts" the children need to know are that the world is full of wonder and diversity and that they are a part of this wonderful world. There are innumerable experiences which can reinforce these facts. Young children can be trusted to discover the ones that best carry the message for them as individuals.

Establishing an interactive "nature center" in the classroom is one way to invite children's active exploration and involvement. This nature center should feature objects from the out-of-doors— e.g., pine cones, rocks, twigs, snake skins, bird nests, different types of bark, etc. All of these items should be "touch me" items. To hold the children's interest, new items should be added frequently and be brought in by both the teacher and the children. Blocks of wood and sanding paper are examples of what can be included in an interactive center. The children can explore the texture of the wood, act on the wood by sanding it, and in the process, discover the beauty of the grain.

Other areas, too should feature hands-on opportunities for nature exploration. The art center could include a variety of "nature items". Small shells, seeds, dried grasses and leaves—all make wonderful materials for creating a collage. The outdoor play area should offer inviting opportunities for fun in nature—not just climbers, swings, and slides. Provide the children with logs to climb on, bushes to crawl under, and dirt for digging. Then watch the action!

Provide pleasant, memorable experiences. Children develop a lasting interest in learning through experiences that are pleasant and memorable. They get "hooked on learning" once they realize that they can have a good time throughout the learning process.

For this reason, the "Do not touch" approach to nature education will never be successful with preschool children. Young children want to hold and manipulate. They'll reach out to touch and pick the wildflowers. Because picking wildflowers isn't the ecologically-correct thing to do, it's important to give young children hands-on learning alternatives. To "Just say no" will leave them feeling frustrated and uninvolved. The challenge is to offer appropriate avenues of engagement and involvement.

In the case of the wildflowers, we might invite the children to explore the flowers through their sense of sight and smell. We might have them lie face-up on the ground right next to their flower of choice. How does the flower look when viewed from the perspective of an ant? How does it smell when sprayed with a sprinkling of water? Where is the best place to stand or sit or kneel to take a picture of the flower to share with Mom or Dad?

Nature appreciation activities for young children must be fun. Unless children can appreciate (and enjoy) the activities themselves, they will not appreciate the object or idea we're attempting to introduce. The enjoyment of experiences in nature is what will lead young children to appreciate nature itself.

Teachers would do well, then, to expend as much thought and energy in considering the "enjoyment factor" of a nature-related experience as they do in the "content factor". To be avoided are situations calling for a long list of reminders and rules. Also to be avoided are too many specific "learning objectives". While children need to know and respect the kinds of behaviors which harm the environment and each other's enjoyment of the environment, they also need to know that it's OK to just sit in the grass and enjoy the world around them. If there are too many directives and too many facts to be learned, the affective and aesthetic aspects of the experience are likely to be lost.

When working with young children, it's also extremely important to keep the activities from getting too complex. If an outdoor excursion or a visit by a traveling zoo involves too many cautions, steps and new experiences, the "pleasantness" of the event quickly becomes jeopardized. Better to provide a simple, uncomplicated experience than to risk overloading both teacher and children in the complexity of the situation.

Emphasize experiencing versus teaching. For effective learning, young children need to be involved in sharing and doing versus listening and watching. They need to explore, experiment, and follow their own curiosity. The teacher's role is not to give the children information, but to provide opportunities for them to experience the richness of the natural world.

Children are naturally curious. They seek information about their environment and, if encouraged, actively engage in experimentation with materials in the world around them. The effective teacher will encourage children to experiment, explore, and get into things that are safe.

The effective teacher will understand that when children ask "What's that?", they aren't always looking for the name of something. What they're often looking for is more information about what they see or are experiencing. The effective teacher will realize that by providing a one-word answer to the question of "What's that?", they may be limiting both the observation and the conversation. What teachers can do instead is to pose other questions for the children to consider— questions to which the children can seek their own answers. Examples: Is it alive? What is it doing? How does it move? Do you see its eyes, nose, mouth, or ears? How does it eat? Where does it live? Does it leave a trail?

Involve full use of the senses. In getting to know the world of nature, young children learn best by experiencing nature versus talking about it. Their mode of engagement with the natural world must be at the sensorimotor level; that is, they must be engaged through their senses and through motoric manipulation. It's important to go outdoors and feel it, smell it, and listen to it, rather than just talk about it. The one sense that must be used with caution in the out-of-doors is that of taste. Some plants are poisonous and children should never be encouraged to taste non-food things. Tasting when outdoors should be limited to known fruits and vegetables. Even this should be done with caution, because of chemicals that may have been sprayed on the plants.

Children need many and varied opportunities for sensing the natural world. "Immersing techniques" are sometimes used to help children become sensorily more in touch with the natural world. A list of "immersing techniques" suggested by Van Matre (1990) include:
- Take off some articles of clothing to increase physical contact.
- Crawl or roll or float instead of walk.
- Get off the path, go cross-country.
- Simulate natural processes (e.g., flow like the water, leap like the wind).
- Block the sense of sight or sound to heighten the other senses.
- Pet and hug and kiss things in the world of nature.

Immersing techniques not only help children see, hear, taste, touch, and smell the world of nature, but also help them tap into a sixth sense as well. This sixth sense is intuition and is often overlooked in discussions about experiencing the world through one's senses. Intuition is the sense which helps a child really "feel" the out-of-doors and to quite literally "absorb" its various moods. Intuition is the direct or immediate perception of truths, facts, etc., without reasoning. Van Matre (1972, 1990) links intuition with "acclimatization," and describes it as a sense of relationship with the earth.

Acclimatization, immersion, intuition—each, in its own way, can help a child feel at home with the world of nature. But intuition, as an avenue for getting to know the natural world, needs to be encouraged and respected. A child's declaration about having heard the wind whisper her name or feeling the rain kiss her cheek should never be dismissed. Nature has the power to touch us in a variety of ways, and these ways warrant respect.

Provide multimodal learning experiences. The professional literature in both early childhood education and environmental education (Bredekamp, 1987; Harlan, 1992; Priest, 1986) addresses the importance of multimodal learning—that is, learning through more than one avenue or channel of information. Multimodal learning is extremely important in nature education for preschoolers. Consider, for example, how young children might learn about flowers. One way is to describe a flower as being made up of different parts with differing functions. This way suggests that children learn by listening and restricts their learning about a flower to a cognitive or rational way of knowing. Through this way of knowing, children can learn the facts about a flower without ever seeing a flower!

There are, of course, many other ways of learning about a flower and additional dimensions to experience. A child can learn about a flower through the use of his or her senses (i.e., by seeing, smelling, and feeling) or by physically examining its differing parts (i.e., the stem, roots, petals, etc.). A child can also learn about a flower through art, literature, and cultural customs (e.g., presenting a flower to someone you love on Valentine's Day). Another way of knowing a flower is to understand its relationship to an entire ecosystem. Children need to know that a flower does not (and cannot) exist in isolation. Each flower depends on and contributes to the greater world of nature. Knowing that "when you pick a flower you trouble a star" can add immensely to an understanding and appreciation of the natural world.

Multimodal learning not only helps children learn about the world around them, but also helps them learn about themselves and fosters development across domains. Self esteem, for example, is closely linked to exploration and discovery. "Finding out" helps children feel competent and triggers a desire to learn more. The pleasure experienced in discovering something in the environment that is awesome, delightful, or comforting also fosters the aesthetic, affective and cognitive growth of the young child (Harlan, 1992).

Teachers can encourage multimodal learning in a variety of ways. One way is by showing respect for "spontaneous demonstrations of children's intuitive and rational thought working together" (Harlan, 1992, p. 8). Children offering their own versions of why certain events occur in the natural world may provide examples of the pairing of intuitive and rationale thinking. A child may describe the sudden movement of a breeze through the leaves as the tree's attempt to wave goodbye. While a "teacher-like" tendency may be to provide some factual information about wind behavior, an "educator" may seize the opportunity to encourage the children to wave back. The "teacher" may be skilled and interested in giving information; the "educator", however, focuses on drawing out from the student his or her own abilities, insights, and understandings.

Focus on relationships. Early childhood education is about relationships, which include peers, adults, materials and the natural surroundings (Bredekamp, 1987). Environmental education is also "a matter of relationships" and includes involvement with, not only the natural world, but people and society, as well (Priest, 1986). Four different types of relationships which should be considered in the development of an environmental education program for preschoolers are interpersonal, intrapersonal, ecosystemic, and ekistic. Following is a discussion of each.

Interpersonal refers to relationships between people. Cooperation, communication, and trust play key roles in the development of interpersonal relationships. Each of these areas is critical to the social development of the young child. Interesting that these same skills have been identified as desired outcomes of an environmental education program (Crompton & Sellar, 1981). The power, or magic, of the outdoor setting includes the tendency to build positive relationships between people (Crompton & Sellar, 1981; Henderson, 1990). Teachers would do well to tap into this aspect of the natural world. One way of doing so is by encouraging cooperative learning experiences in the out-of-doors. Children can be paired with partners for a variety of activities, including scavenger hunts, blindfold walks, litter patrol, etc.

Intrapersonal refers to how one relates to self. Locus of control, level of independence, and self concept are all important aspects of one's intrapersonal relationship. Both early childhood education and environmental education have proven effective in fostering intrapersonal relationships (Crompton & Sellar, 1981; Henderson, 1990; Spodek, Saracho, & Davis, 1987).

Teachers can use the natural environment to foster the development of healthy intrapersonal relationships in young children. Examples of how this might be done include:
- involving children in anti-litter campaigns, where they can experience the satisfaction of making a real contribution in saving Planet Earth
- involving children in the care of plants and animals, where what they do contributes to the well being of other living things
- helping children become aware of their natural kinship with other living and nonliving things
- helping children feel comfortable in the out-of-doors, thus enhancing their self confidence, sense of independence, and enjoyment.

Helping children feel comfortable in the out-of-doors should focus on both the emotional and physical realms. Feeling comfortable emotionally includes understanding that the weather and seasons change; that wind, thunder, and lightning are natural phenomena; and much of what we experience in nature is predictable. Feeling comfortable physically includes dressing for the weather—layering in the winter, protecting self against the sun in summer, etc.

Ecosystemic refers to the interdependence of all parts of an ecosystem. A major goal of environmental education is to increase awareness and understanding of the dynamic relationship that exists between all living and nonliving organisms. This awareness and understanding needs to occur in both the cognitive and affective domains of learning. A desired outcome of an environmental education program is the understanding that there is an "interdependent web" that connects all aspects of the natural world.

Ekistic refers to the interaction between people and their surroundings. The development of an ekistic relationship promotes a sense of what is "right" or ethical and encourages respect for one's surroundings. As environmental problems continue to mount, the human/Earth relationship undoubtedly takes on serious moral considerations. While preschool children should not be overly burdened with feelings of responsibility for the state of the environment, they can and should realize that they are a part of (vs. separate from) the natural world.

Young children learn values and ethics by watching the significant people around them. The teacher, as a role model, plays an especially important part in values education (Caduto, 1983). Teachers, demonstrating care for the environment, are contributing to the development of healthy ekistic relationships.

While young children may not be able to fully understand why they should be concerned with abuse and neglect of the environment, they are old enough to appreciate the beauty of nature and begin developing some ecologically-sound behaviors. The following simple rules would be appropriate for young children:

- Take care of plants and other living things.
- Keep the air, the water, and the Earth clean and free from pollution.
- Respect the lives of animals and humans alike.
- Use only what you need.
- Plant flowers and trees.
- Pick up trash.

Demonstrate a personal interest in and enjoyment of the natural world. The teacher's authentic interest and enjoyment are critical to the success of an early childhood environmental education program, for it is the teacher's own sense of wonder which will ignite and sustain the young child's love of nature.

Teachers with a minimum background in science, sometimes feel intimidated about teaching environmental education to young children. Such teachers can feel at ease, because it is not scientific information that is most needed in an environmental education program for preschoolers. Feelings are far more important than facts when it comes to introducing children to the world of nature. Once again, Rachel Carson's (1956) words are pertinent: "I sincerely believe that for the child, and for the parent [or teacher] seeking to guide him, it is not half so important to know as to feel" (p. 45).

Teachers can demonstrate interest in and enjoyment of the natural world in many different ways including the following:
- bringing into the classroom items from nature (e.g., pine cones, fresh flowers, shiny pebbles, snake skins, etc.)
- growing plants from seeds
- displaying books and pictures depicting the beauty and wonders of the natural environment
- taking time outdoors to examine different types of plants, rocks, trees, insects, etc.
- having and caring for classroom pets
- inviting naturalists into the classroom to share information about nature
- taking field trips to "natural" places (meadows, forests, streams, etc.)
- decorating the classroom with items from nature (driftwood, dried flowers, house plants, etc.)
- setting up and caring for a bird feeder outside the classroom window
- planting a tree or bush in the school yard.

Most teachers realize that young children learn more about attitudes and values from their observations of adults' behaviors, than they do from what adults say to them. If an adult takes the time to watch a butterfly move from flower to flower, or a squirrel eat the corn from a cob thrown out on the school lawn, children's curiosity and respect are likely to be aroused. If, however, the teacher walks right by and never seems to notice the beauty and wonder of nature, the children are likely to dismiss the sounds, sights, and feel of nature as having little importance. It is the teacher's enthusiasm and interest in nature—more than his or her scientific knowledge about the natural world—that will make the greatest difference in sparking the curiosity and interest of young children.

Teachers can show enthusiasm and interest in nature by stopping to look, to feel, and to listen. They can kneel on the ground and put their face in the grass to enjoy the scent of a wildflower growing there They can use a magnifying glass to examine the many colors of a small pebble found at the edge of a creek, and they can stand looking toward the sky as a flock of birds makes its way south for the winter.

Once a teacher demonstrates a sense of wonder and a respect for nature, these same qualities are likely to be "caught" by the children. Much of what we want children to learn or develop as they move through their early childhood years is not so much taught, as it is caught. Feelings of wonder and appreciation for the natural world certainly fall in the realm of what is primarily caught versus taught.

Model caring for the natural environment. In addition to demonstrating interest in and enjoyment of the natural world, it's also important for teachers to model a sense of caring. "Do as I say and not as I do" is a poor maxim for fostering ecologically-responsible behaviors. Children need to see the teacher demonstrate care for the environment, before they will follow the teacher's exhortations about being caretakers of the Earth. Caring for the environment can be demonstrated in a number of ways that are understandable to young children. Many such ways are outlined in the book, *50 Simple Things You Can do to Save the Earth* (Earthworks Group, 1989). Examples include:

- **conserving water.** Times when this might be modeled with young children in the classroom include washing dishes and brushing teeth.
- **recycling packaging** (e.g., paper bags, boxes, Styrofoam trays, etc.). Packaging can often be re-used for projects or storage within the classroom.
- **recycling pop cans and paper.** Students can assist in the collection and sorting of items that can be sold or donated to recycling firms or organizations.

Another powerful way to model caring for the environment is through gentleness in behavior. People who care do not break branches on trees or bushes, avoid picking wildflowers, and step over or around ants, insects, and caterpillars. People who care also demonstrate a sense of responsibility — they clean up after themselves and try to avoid damaging the environment in any way. They operate from the model of "Let it be" in relation to such things as bird nests, ant hills, wildflowers, and such.

Maintain a warm, accepting, and nurturing atmosphere. Young children learn best in an environment that is warm and accepting. They need to know that they are valued and that they can trust the adults who work with them. A close rapport between child and teacher is essential for the child to feel supported in his or her efforts to explore and experiment.

A warm, accepting, and nurturing atmosphere is also important to maintain consistency between how we teach and what we teach. "A child who learns that he or she is valuable ... is more likely to pick up litter, avoid stepping on plants or destroying animals' homes, conserve energy and generally care for Earth and its creatures" (Caduto & Bruchac, 1991, p. 7).

Introduce multicultural experiences and perspectives. Every culture has its own gifts to bring to an environmental education program. Such gifts can often be gleaned from works of literature and art. Some professional resource books are also available. Two highly recommended books are *Keepers of the Animals* and *Keepers of the Earth*. These two books feature Native American stories and wildlife activities. They're authored by Michael Caduto and Joseph Bruchac (1991) and come with a teacher's guide.

Another way to introduce multicultural experiences and perspectives is through visitors to the classroom. Individuals from a variety of cultures could be invited to share their experiences with and understandings about the natural world. Invited visitors may include veterinarians, naturalists, farmers, gardeners, etc. Books and pictures of individuals from different ethnic groups engaged in conservation or other nature-related activities could also enhance cultural diversity in the classroom.

Focus on the beauty and wonder of nature. Children can learn many different things about the natural world. They can learn about nature as a "resource" for people; they can learn that air, water, and sunlight are important to all living things; that elements of the earth can be divided between living and nonliving things; etc. But the most important thing that young children can learn about the earth is that it is full of beauty and wonder. It is a sense of wonder which will prove to be one of the strongest and most enduring incentives for saving Planet Earth. It is also a sense of wonder which will add immeasurably to one's enjoyment and appreciation of life.

Go outside whenever possible. Studies indicate that children in the United States spend over 95% of their time indoors and that, by the end of their high school experience, they will have spent 18,000 hours in the classroom (Cohen, 1984). Additionally, by the year 2000, over 90% of all Americans will live in urban areas (Schicker, 1988). Is it any wonder, then, that many children know so little about the natural world and even feel a sense of alienation from the world of nature?

Young children tend to bond with, or develop an emotional attachment for, what is familiar and comfortable to them. If they are to develop a sense of love and caring for the natural world, they must be given time to experience the out-of-doors; time to get to know it as a place of wonder, comfort, and joy; and time to experience it as their home (i.e., the place where they live). To know the beauty and warmth of the sun, they must stand outdoors on a sunny day. To know the magic and wonder of an apple tree in bloom, they need time to observe the swelling and bursting of the buds. Such experiences—and such "knowing"—cannot come by way of words or pictures. Such knowing comes only by way of experience.

Infuse environmental education into all aspects of the early childhood program. Environmental education should not be an "add on" to what is already being offered in educational programs. It should, instead, be integrated into all aspects of the program. This is called the "infusion approach" and is highly recommended in the environmental education literature (Disinger, 1985/86; Ramsey, Hungerford,& Volk, 1992).

The "infusion approach" also matches best practices in early childhood education. Educational programs for young children should not be divided into different subject areas, but should provide experiences which promote development and understanding across domains and areas of study (Bredekamp, 1987). Curriculum for young children can be defined as "everything the young child experiences"—this includes the physical arrangement of the classroom, the materials used to decorate the classroom, the food the children have for lunch or snack, the way people interact with each other, the toys and other learning materials available for the children, and the nature of the outdoor play area.

Implementation Guidelines

To make environmental education a part of an early childhood program, no new areas need be added. In fact, to be optimally effective, environmental education should be infused into every aspect of the early childhood program. The following "implementation guidelines" are offered as ways in which this might be accomplished and are based on a recent review of the literature on children and ecology (Cohen, 1992). These same implementation guidelines, with specific examples on how to actualize them, are discussed throughout the remainder of this guide.

1. Introduce nature-related materials and activities in the different learning centers.
2. Make animals and plants a part of the classroom environment.
3. Share pro-nature books with children.
4. Encourage nature-related art activities.
5. Introduce nature-related music and movement activities.
6. Celebrate each of the seasons with special nature-related activities.
7. Demonstrate the connection between the food we eat and the world of nature.
8. Introduce a variety of nature-related themes and concepts through group activities.
9. Display nature-related art and use materials from the natural world to decorate the classroom.
10. Go on a variety of nature-study field trips.
11. Introduce children to wildlife and other aspects of nature in and around the school yard.
12. Individualize the program to meet special needs and interests.
13. Invite parent participation in nature-related activities.
14. Enhance your own understanding and appreciation of the natural world.

PART II
Implementing the Curriculum

*"The years of early childhood are
the time to prepare the soil."*

Rachael Carson

"There was a time when . . . the world was a song and the song was exciting."
From Les Misearbles

Chapter 4
Indoor Discoveries

Learning Centers: Bringing the Outdoors In

Implementation Guideline #1: Introduce nature-related materials and activities in the different learning centers.

Basic Centers

Many early childhood classrooms feature "learning centers" as the primary vehicle for child-initiated learning experiences. Learning centers are sometimes referred to as "interest centers" and are arranged to support major learning functions across the different developmental domains (i.e. language development, gross and fine motor development, social development, etc.). For maximum effectiveness, learning centers should be clearly-defined areas within the classroom. To achieve this, small cupboards, tables, or screens can be used to create "small rooms" for each center. Each center can then be labeled with a mobile or sign hung at the children's eye level. Once the basic learning centers are set up, additional materials can be added for variety and enrichment purposes.

Following is a discussion about basic learning centers often found in an early childhood classroom and the type of materials usually included.

1. Language Experience Center

This center is sometimes referred to as the "book corner" or "literacy center." It is usually located in a quiet area of the room and is designed to foster a sense of comfort and relaxation. In addition to books, the language experience center may include magazines, catalogs, puppets, flannelboard materials, pre-recorded audiotapes and tape player with head phones, and materials for writing. It may also include pillows, rugs, and a rocking chair.

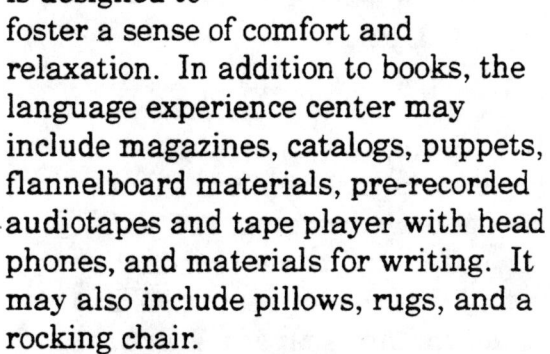

2. Manipulative Center

Materials in the manipulative center encourage children to learn about relationships involving size, space, and shape. Materials in this center can also help children learn about cause and effect and give children many opportunities to practice fine motor skills. Puzzles, pegboards, and different types of "busy boxes" are often found in the manipulative center. Child-sized tables and chairs make it easier for children to work with the materials in this center.

3. Block Center

Blocks of different sizes and shapes are always available in the block center. Accessories are often added to enhance pretend play. Such accessories might include small toy cars or animals, miniature road signs, and people figurines. To maximize child safety and freedom in building elaborate and not-so-elaborate structures (e.g., roads, buildings, animal pens, etc.), the block center is best located out of the flow of traffic.

4. Texture Table

While texture tables are often used for water or sand play, they may be used to introduce a variety of other sensory materials as well. Texture tables may be filled with beans, rice, popped and/or unpopped popcorn, peanuts in the shell, snow, leaves, etc. Cups, funnels, hand shovels and rakes, large spoons, bottles, and sifters may be added to invite active exploration and experimentation on the part of the children.

5. Art Center

This center usually features crayons, felt-tipped markers, paints, pencils, scissors, different sizes and shapes of paper, tape, glue, and yarn. Painting easels and chalk boards may also be found in the art center. Old magazines and newspaper ads are sometimes included for cutting and pasting activities. The art center is often located close to a water source and in an area where the floor covering is easy to clean. In addition to the easels, other furniture in the art center often includes child-sized tables and chairs.

6. Music Center

The music center offers opportunities for both listening to and making music. A tape player and pre-recorded music allow children to choose favorite songs for listening. Blank tapes invite children to record their own voices and original " rhythm band" music. A variety of rhythm band instruments encourage children to experiment with different sounds and rhythmic patterns.

7. Dramatic Play Center

While dramatic play centers are often set up as kitchen corners, they may also feature other pretend-play situations. Popular themes found in dramatic play centers include supermarket, post office, doctor's office, and McDonald's.

8. Science Center or Discovery Center

The science center often includes materials relating to the natural environment. It may also includes tools to facilitate exploration and discovery, such as a magnifying glass and scales.

9. Math Center

A math center usually offers a variety of materials for weighing, measuring, comparing lengths, counting, etc. Tools for doing so are also included. These may include rulers of different types, scales, clocks, and thermometers.

Adding Nature-Related Materials

Teachers interested in helping children learn more about the natural world will find that learning centers can serve as an excellent vehicle for bringing the world of nature into the classroom. A listing of the typical learning centers and some suggestions on the type of nature-related materials that might be added is presented on page 30.

Criteria of Appropriateness

In bringing the outdoors in through learning center materials, it's important for teachers to keep the criteria of appropriateness in mind. To determine the appropriateness of different nature-related materials, teachers may ask: Can these materials be used quite naturally and safely by young children? Small, smooth pebbles, for example, may not be appropriate for the texture table if children in the classroom tend to put things in their mouth. Similarly, animals that bite or scratch should not be chosen as classroom pets, as children will naturally want to hold and feed the pet.

The most appropriate materials are those which the children can safely feel and manipulate and which they find interesting. Some twigs, for example, are more interesting than others. A twig with a beaver's teeth marks will capture the children's interest much more readily than a twig with no such markings on it. Similarly, a branch with buds ready to burst into bloom will add more beauty and variety to the classroom than a branch which is dead.

Recommended Resources

Avoiding Infusion Confusion: A Practical Handbook for Infusing Environmental Activities into your Classroom. H. Hayden, M. Oltman, R. Thompson-Tucker, S. Wood. Amherst Junction, WI: Central Wisconsin Environmental Station, 1987.

Creative Environmental Education Activities for Children. Environmental Education Curriculum Guide. Tennessee Valley Authority (Land Between the Lakes). Golden Pond, KY: TVA, 1984.

Teaching Activities in Environmental Education. (Volumes 2 & 3). J. Wheatley & H. Coon. Columbus, OH: ERIC Clearinghouse for Science, Mathematics, and Environmental Education. 1974, 1975.

The Outside Play and Learning Book. K. Miller. Mt. Rainier, MD: Gryphon House, 1989.

Mud, Sand, and Water. D. Hill. Washington, D.C.: Minnesota Department of Education, 1977.

Bubbles, Rainbows, and Worms: Science Experiments for Preschool Children. S. Brown. Mt. Rainier, MD: Gryphon House, Inc., 1981.

Mudpies to Magnets. E. Sherwood, R. Williams, & R. Rockwell. Mt. Rainier, MD: Gryphon House, 1987.

More Mudpies to Magnets. E. Sherwood, R. Williams, & R. Rockwell. Mt. Rainier, Gryphon House, 1990.

Suggested Children's Book

Robbins, Ken. *A FLOWER GROWS.* Photos by author. Dial, 1990. Nonfiction. Interest Level: Ages 4-8.

Learning Center	Nature-Related Materials
Language Experience Center	books and pictures about nature, animal puppets, flannel board animal characters, audio tapes with songs about nature
Manipulative Center	puzzles relating to nature, small animal figurines, shells of different sizes and shapes
Block Center	pebbles, pieces of bark, pine cones, dry wood
Texture Table	pine cones, leaves in fall, snow, shells, pebbles, magnifying glass, small toy animals
Art Center	pine cones, small leaves, twigs, tree bark (for rubbings), a variety of seeds, leaves, acorns, dried grasses
Music Center	records and tapes featuring sounds **of** and **about** nature; natural materials for making homemade instruments (e.g., shakers from seeds and potato chip cans)
Dramatic Play Center	camping equipment, child-sized gardening tools, materials for a pet store or veterinary office, stuffed animals and puppets
Science Center	aquarium, terrarium, caged classroom animals, plants, dried grasses, seeds, abandoned bird's nest, fall leaves, skin of a snake or cicada, picture books relating to the items in the center, photographs depicting changes throughout the seasons, wood and plants at different stages, blocks of wood and sand paper
Math Center	natural objects (shells, rocks, feathers, etc.) to count, weigh, and measure

Animals and Plants in the Classroom

Implementation Guideline # 2: Make animals and plants a part of the classroom environment

Animals in the Classroom

Having animals in the classroom is a challenging, fun, and rewarding experience. The opportunity to study animals at close range sets the stage for many interesting and stimulating learning experiences. Children are fascinated by animals and will, on their own, take the time to observe the characteristics and behaviors of classroom animals. They'll ask questions, beg to be involved in the care and feeding process, and never tire of observing changes in what the animal does and how it looks.

Such active involvement fosters development of the young child in a number of different ways. Objects of interest always encourage observational and language skills. Involvement in the care of another living thing fosters a sense of stewardship and responsibility. It also encourages the development of a positive attitude toward the world of nature.

There are many different animals that can be kept successfully in the early childhood classroom and provide the children with valuable learning experiences. There are some guidelines, however, that need to be followed to ensure the success of the experience.

Planning is the first step in the process. Attention to this step will increase the likelihood of meaningful learning experiences for the children and ensure the welfare of the animal involved. During the planning process, the following questions should be addressed:

1. What type of animal should I select?
2. Where should I get the animal?
3. What type of environment does the animal need?
4. What's involved in the care and feeding of the animal? (e.g., What does it eat?; When does it sleep?; How will it get the exercise it needs?; etc.)
5. Is it safe for the children to handle this animal?
6. What will I do with the animal after the project is over (or during the summer, etc.)?
7. Are there any legal considerations related to the confinement of the animal?

Selecting animals. The first, and probably the most important, decision to be made in planning for a classroom animal is selecting the type of animal to have. Factors to be considered in making this decision should include the health and safety of the children, the health and daily care of the animal, legal limitations, and housing and space requirements of the animal. Following is an additional set of generalizations, developed by David Kramer in *Animals in the Classroom* (1989, p. 5), which should also be considered.

1. Smaller animals are generally better than larger ones.
2. Local animals are generally better than exotic ones.
3. Wild mammals should not be kept in the classroom.
4. Venomous animals should not be kept in the classroom.
5. Sick or injured animals should not be kept in the classroom.
6. No animal should be kept in the classroom unless:

- it is hardy and can thrive in captivity
- its natural habitat can be duplicated there
- its normal behavior can be expressed in the enclosure
- it can adjust to the normal classroom environment
- it can be properly cared for over weekends

Some animals can be collected locally from their natural habitats (e.g., earthworms, spiders, tadpoles, insects). Others can be purchased from pet stores or biological supply companies. Several such companies are listed in Appendix A. In making decisions about which animals to introduce into the classroom for observation or as pets, teachers may wish to refer to the following information.

Selecting Classroom Animals

Animals	Characteristics	Collecting and Maintaining
Earthworms	No internal or external skeleton; soft; fleshy; body made up of segments (rings); live in soil (may surface, if ground becomes very wet); benefit the soil by mixing it and keeping it loose and by releasing nutrients into it.	Live under the soil and not often seen. Can be found by digging in the ground or turning over logs; also found above ground after heavy rain. Can be kept in food storage containers (milk carton, butter tubs, etc.) partially filled with moist soil. Lid with holes for ventilation can be used to avoid escapes. Larger container should be used if worms are to be kept for more than a day or two. An aquarium would accommodate several dozen worms and would provide some underground viewing. Place 8 to 10 inches of soil mixed with compost or sawdust in the container. Add water to keep the soil moist (not wet). Sprinkle bits of grass, dried leaves, apple or potato peelings, and coffee grounds for food. May also sprinkle grass seed on surface and grow grass for natural food.

Animals	Characteristics	Collecting and Maintaining
Crayfish	Crayfish are usually about 2 to 5 inches in length. Their bodies are divided into two parts-head area and abdomen area. Crayfish have two pairs of antennae and five pairs of legs. They have sharp claws, or pincers, on their front pair of legs. Crayfish use their pincers for eating, protecting themselves and where they live, and digging. They use their other legs for walking. Crayfish can walk forward, backward, and sideways. They move around in the water and on land. They spend most of their time on the bottom of streams, rivers, ponds, and lakes. Some types of crayfish dig down to water in damp areas. Their dig sites can be found by looking for a mound (or "chimney") of mud balls above the ground. These mounds are usually one to three inches high. Crayfish eat snails, small fish, tadpoles, or the young of insects. They also eat some types of plants. Crayfish will eat both living and dead plant and animal materials. They are more active at nightfall and at daybreak. The female crayfish lays eggs in late summer or fall. These eggs become attached to her body. After the eggs hatch, the young crayfish remain attached to their mother's body for one or two weeks, before living on their own. Young crayfish shed their skin several times before they become adults.	Crayfish are easy to catch, purchase, and maintain. They must be handled very carefully, however, as their pincers are sharp. A large net or some bait on the end of a string can be used for catching crayfish. Because crayfish will use their pincers to grab the bait, no hook is needed when fishing for them. Crayfish can often be found near loose rocks in shallow streams. When the rocks are moved, the crayfish will usually attempt to escape. Crayfish can also be purchased from bait shops and biological supply companies (See Appendix A). An aquarium makes an appropriate home for a crayfish in the classroom. No more than one or two crayfish should be put in a single aquarium. Add some aquarium gravel, several small rocks, a few aquatic plants, and one to two inches of water. Feed the crayfish small pieces of meat or fish and vegetables. Clean their cage often and avoid letting uneaten food remain in the water for very long. Crayfish will do fine on their own over weekends and short vacations, if they have aquatic plants in their cage. Under careful supervision, crayfish can be handled safely by the children. Crayfish do not bite but do pinch with their claws. Crayfish can be picked up by grasping the abdomen area above their walking legs. They should not be kept out of the water for more than ten minutes at a time, as they need the water to breathe.

Animals	Characteristics	Collecting and Maintaining
Aquatic Snails	There are many different types of snails. Some live in the water; others live on land. Many snails have spiral shells which live and grow with their bodies. Snails with shells withdraw into their shells for protection.	Easy to collect and maintain. Can be found in or on submerged vegetation in a pond. Collect pond vegetation and pond water with the snails. Handle snails very gently, putting them in a container with pond water as soon as possible. Local pet stores also carry aquatic snails and plants. Use an aquarium or other large wide-mouthed container to make a home for the snails. Add sand on the bottom, aquatic plants anchored in the sand, pond water to within about four inches of the top, and cover which will permit air exchange. Maintain the snails by adding small amounts of fish food and additional pond water when needed. Aged tap water (water left to stand in an open container for 24 hours) can also be used.

For more information about the characteristics and care of classroom animals, refer to *Animals in the Classroom* by David Kramer. Also, soon to be available is *Nature Education Guide for Pre-school Teachers,* by Richard Cohen and Betty Tunick. This guide presents ideas for establishing mini-habitats in the classroom. It is presently being field tested through Pacific Oaks College and Children's Programs in Pasadena, California.

Providing a place for the animal. Deciding where the classroom animal should be kept is another important decision to be made. While the needs and comfort of the animal should be one of the major considerations in making this decision, opportunities for children to observe the animal should also be considered. If the cage, itself, is not transparent, it should have a window or other type of viewing arrangements.

While some types of animals require a more specialized environment, a screen-covered aquarium can often be used as a multi-purpose cage. For certain very small animals (e.g., insects), a screen-covered jar will be sufficient. Factors to think about in choosing a place for the animal to live include adequate exercise space, good ventilation, a place to hide, security against escape, easy maintenance (cleaning, providing food and water, etc.).

Taking care of the animal. In caring for an animal, it's extremely important to know about the animal's food, water, rest, and exercise needs. Classroom animals should be offered their natural foods, as much as possible. If this cannot be obtained from the natural environment, a pet store, bait shop, or biological supply company may have what the animal needs. (See Appendix A for a list of biological supply companies.)

Keeping the animal and its surroundings clean is another important aspect of caring for a classroom animal. A clean, pleasant environment is important both for the welfare of the animal and for the lesson it demonstrates to the children about respect for the natural world.

Some animals require more day-to-day care than others. It's important to consider the care requirements in the process of selecting a classroom animal and avoid those animals which require more special attention than what is manageable in the classroom. Children should be involved in the care whenever possible, but always under careful supervision.

Saying good-by to the animal. How long animals should be kept in the classroom depends, to a large extent, on the type of animal involved and the purpose for which the animal was selected. Wild animals should be chosen very carefully and never be kept for more than several weeks. Other common-pet animals (e.g., hamsters, pet mice, gerbils, etc.) can be kept for longer periods of time. No animal, however, should be kept beyond the time that children are interested and/or care begins to slack.

Teachers are sometimes faced with the concern of what to do with a classroom animal when it's time to say good-by. As a general rule, children should be involved in the process of finding a new home for the animal (or returning it to its natural habitat). Through this process, the children can learn many valuable lessons about how to relate to the natural world in a responsible and caring way.

Classroom animals can be released into the natural environment only if they were collected from the area and conditions (weather, etc.) have not changed significantly. If the animal is not from the area, the natural environment may not provide the needed food and shelter and the animal may then suffer and die.

An animal can sometimes be given to someone else who will care for it—a parent, another teacher, or other interested person. Some pet stores will consider taking a healthy animal. The classroom pet should never be sent home with a child, unless the parents are knowledgeable about the animal's needs and have expressed interest in caring for the animal.

Dos and don'ts about classroom animals.
The following list of dos and don'ts are provided to help ensure the children's safety and the animal's welfare. When in doubt about what is safe or appropriate, consult a naturalist.

- Check school regulations regarding animals in the classroom.
- Check federal and state regulations regarding the collection and confinement of animals. These guidelines are usually available through the state Department of Natural Resources, Division of Wildlife.
- Choose animals that allow children to be involved in the care and feeding process.
- Help children feel comfortable around the animal.
- Instruct children to wash their hands before and after feeding or handling the animals and after cleaning their cages.
- Provide prompt medical attention in the event a child is bitten, scratched, or stung.
- Find out about how to best take care of the animal.
- Treat the animal with respect at all times.
- Inform parents about the presence of the animal.
- Don't allow children to pick up animals to bring into the classroom.
- Don't allow the children to tease or torment the animal.

Plants in the Classroom

Cut flowers, house plants, dried grasses, and newly-developing seedlings can all add interest and beauty to the classroom environment and help young children grow in understanding and appreciation of the world of nature. Following are some suggestions on how to make plants a regular part of the classroom environment.

- Invite the children to bring in cuttings from houseplants they have at home (with Mom's permission, of course!). Keep these in a glass of water until roots appear. Plant them in a terrarium or flower pot.
- Start plants from seeds and from bulbs.

- Practice recycling when planting. Use meat trays, yogurt containers, egg cartons, etc. as containers for planting seeds and seedlings.
- Grow some plants that can be transplanted outdoors. Include both flowers and vegetable plants.
- Have children water the plants with a small spray bottle. This helps prevent over watering.
- Display pictures and books of plants. Include pictures of plants that grow in different areas, such as the dessert, a mountain side, woodland, pond, etc.

Suggested Children's Book

Mazer, Anne. *THE SALAMANDER ROOM*. Illustrations by Steve Johnson. Knopf, 1991. Fiction. Interest Level: Ages 3-7.

Recommended Resources

Animals in the Classroom. D. Kramer. New York: Addison Wesley, 1989.

Earth Child. K. Sheehan, & M. Waidner. Tulsa, OK: Council Oak Books, 1991. Chapter 8 Hurt No Living Thing

Books and Stories

Implementation Guideline #3: Share pro-nature books with children.

Alternatives to the Big Bad Wolf*

Children and adults often associate the words "story time" with feelings of closeness, comfort, and excitement. Story time means a time of togetherness in thoughts and feelings, as well as in physical space. Exploring the wonder and mystery of stories together can establish bonds of caring and understanding between the reader and listener. But there is yet another dimension to story time that merits serious consideration—that is, the development of concepts, attitudes, and values.

From preschool through adulthood, stories can also serve as a powerful medium for shaping one's way of thinking and believing. This aspect of stories, however, is probably the most influential during the early childhood years. Teachers and parents would do well, then, to select with care the types of books they read and make available to young children.

Not all books portray the kinds of attitudes and values we'd like to instill in our young children. One area of concern has to do with the way the natural world is portrayed. Some children's books suggest that the natural world exists to serve the interests of people and that people have the right to use (and exploit) the earth to their own short-term advantage. Other children's books suggest that certain elements of the natural world are evil or "bad." With a growing awareness of how our behaviors are causing ecological disasters, such messages are unacceptable.

There are alternatives to the "big bad wolf syndrome" in children's literature, some of which will be discussed in a following section. Presented first, however, is a brief discussion of the big bad wolf as portrayed in the story of "The Three

---

*NOTE: An earlier version of this section was published in the *Journal of Ohio Elementary Kindergarten Nursery Educators*, Vol. 11, 1991.

Little Pigs". While there are several versions of this story, the wolf in each of the versions is presented as a mean, greedy, frightening creature. The pigs' way of dealing with this creature is to boil him alive in a big iron pot. The story suggests a "we" versus "him" mentality, not too unlike the way in which many people tend to think of and relate to nature. We, as a society of people, tend to see ourselves as "separate from" versus "a part of" the natural world in which we live. We have, in fact, developed a certain prejudice against nature (Cohen, 1984) and tend to think of ourselves as having exploitation rights over the rest of the natural world. Such attitudes are harmful to, not only the natural world outside of ourselves, but also to the development of ourselves as sensitive, caring, wholesome human beings (Burrus-Bammel & Bammel, 1990; Henderson, 1990).

Identifying pro-nature books. While children's books which foster a love for nature seem to be somewhat scarce, some attempts have been made to identify the literature promoting positive attitudes toward the natural world. Following is a brief discussion of some of these books. A more extensive listing is presented in Appendix B. Care was taken to ensure that books on this list meet one or more of the following criteria:

1. present ideas that suggest living in harmony with the natural world versus in competition with or in charge of nature
2. express, in some way, an appreciation and wonder of nature
3. present information or ideas that encourage an attitude of caring about the natural environment.

In choosing pro-nature books, it's important to avoid books which are in conflict with any of the above themes or messages. It's also important to choose books which are well written and of high interest to young children. Following are some examples.

The Very Hungry Caterpillar by Eric Carle presents, in picture book format, the metamorphosis of a butterfly. This book is cleverly written and illustrated, and is designed to instruct and delight the very youngest child. Nature themes presented in this story include excitement, beauty and wonder in relation to the natural world.

The Very Busy Spider, another book by Eric Carle, presents an industrious spider who will not allow herself to be diverted from her task of spinning a web. A number of different farm animals try, but the little spider persists and produces a masterpiece of both beauty and usefulness. Children enjoy this multi-sensory book, where they can feel the pictures as well as see them. They see and feel the spider's web as it grows from a simple line into a complex and beautiful creation. In addition to excitement, beauty and wonder of nature, other nature concepts presented in this book include the connectedness of all things in the natural world—even the humble spider who plays an important role in nature's scheme of things.

Home in the Sky is a book by Jeannie Baker about a homing pigeon who lives on the roof of a building. One morning, after flying away from his flock, he gets caught in a rainstorm but is soon rescued by a young boy who would like to keep him. The pigeon's unerring instincts, however, carry him safely home. Extraordinary lifelike collage illustrations add to the charm of this book. Nature concepts presented in this story include concern for wildlife and feelings of connectedness to the natural world.

The Fall of Freddie the Leaf, by Leo Buscaglia, is a story about Freddie and his companion leaves who change with the passing seasons. Falling to the ground with winter's snow is sure to happen. Before the fall, however, Freddie and his friend, Daniel, have time to discuss the meaning of both life and death. In addition to the life-death paradigm, other nature-related concepts presented in this book are the passing of the seasons and the beauty and wonder of our natural world.

A Tree is Nice, with text by Janice May Udry and illustrations by Marc Simont, outlines many different ways in which our lives are enriched by the trees around us. This book, marked by humor, beauty, and poetic simplicity, is brief but powerful in its invitation to fall in love with nature. The outcome for many readers and listeners is a deeper appreciation of our natural world.

Once There Was a Tree, by Natalia Romanova, is another book about the wonder of trees. In this story, a tree stump attracts many living creatures, including people. When this tree is gone, a new tree takes its place and attracts the same creatures, who are still in need of the gifts the tree has to offer. Outstanding illustrations by Gennady Spirin greatly enhance the book. Nature concepts presented include understandings about time, seasons, and the interdependence of all living creatures.

A House of Leaves, by Kiyoshi Soya, tells the story of young Sarah who seeks shelter from the rain under an umbrella of low hanging leaves. She is soon joined by a praying mantis, a lady bug, and several other woodland creatures. The impact of the story comes with the realization that humans and animals share a common home.

In looking for your own pro-nature books, you might start by asking yourself the following questions:
1. Do the characters in the story show an appreciation for nature and a sense of wonder about the natural world?
2. Do the characters in the story show compassion and empathy for nature, versus trying to dominate and control the natural world?
3. Do the ideas and information presented in the book encourage a sense of caring about the natural environment?
4. Are the ideas and information presented in the book true to the ways of the natural world?

If the answer to one or more of these questions is "yes," you may have found a pro-nature book.

Many children's books are about animals or feature animals as major characters. While it's important for children to be introduced to a variety of animals, it's also important to choose books that present animals in realistic ways. Many children's books do not. According to Thomas A More (1977), children's nature books depict animals in one of three ways. Some animals are presented as people, in that they walk upright and wear clothes. In other books, animals look and behave like animals, but use human speech. A third way in which animals are presented in children's literature is as animals, but animals who are not representative of the way they really are. Bambi is an example. Animals as animals are often presented in sentimental and anthropocentric ways. According to More, books with this type of representation should be avoided, as they are misleading as to what animals are really like.

Big Books

Big Books are usually about 14 inches by 17 inches in size and make reading aloud to a group of children especially rewarding, in that the children can more easily see all the pictures. Some Big Books come with accompanying small books (about 7 inches by 9 inches). One set available through Rigby (P.O. Box 797, Chystal Lake, IL 60014) features a Big Book for each of the four seasons. The set includes, not only the Big Books and small books, but also audio cassettes to accompany each title and teachers' notes. This set is especially rich in the photography used to illustrate each of the seasons. Rigby also publishes Big Book/small book sets featuring the butterfly and tadpole life-cycles, as well as a number of other nature-related topics, including interesting facts about animals, wild animal habitats, dinosaurs, forests, etc.

Multicultural Books

Many native people lived in harmony with nature and valued their close relationship to nature. This spirit of harmony and respect is often reflected in the stories they share with their children. Attempts have been made to identify some of these stories. Following are some children's books reflecting the Native American orientation to the natural world.

Small Wolf. This story by Nathaniel Benchley is about a Native American boy who meets white men on the island of Manhattan and sadly learns that their ideas about land differ from his own. The story presents the Native Americans' point of view in a way appropriate for young children.

Little Runner of the Longhouse. This story by Betty Baker is about Little Runner's experiences during the Iroquois New Year ceremonies. The story provides an interesting combination of child play and background information about Native American life.

Baby Rattlesnake. This book by Te Ata, tells the story of a Southwest Native American family. This and the other two Native American books mentioned above are available through Chaselle, Inc., 9645 Gerwig Lane, Columbia, MD 21046-1503.

The Desert is Theirs. This book by Byrd Baylor explains why the Papago Indians choose to live in a desert. The story demonstrates a peaceful coexistence with the natural environment and provides insights into the lives and legends of the Papago Indians.

Who Speaks for Wolf: A Native American Learning Story. This story by Paula Underwood addresses a conflict between wolves and a Native American tribe when the People seek a new place to live. After realizing that the wolves will neither be frightened away nor bribed with food into leaving on their own, the People struggle with the decision of becoming wolf killers or moving themselves from the land that is rightfully Wolf's. The question of "Who speaks for Wolf?" goes unanswered, as European people arrive, bringing with them a way of thinking and living which is quite different from the Native American way.

The Land of Gray Wolf. In this book, the author, Thomas Locker, tells the story of a piece of land that has endured different types of devastation at the hands of the humans who occupy it. The story presents a Native American perspective and ends on the hopeful note that, in time to come, the land may return to the grandeur and beauty it had before human devastation. Magnificent illustrations by the author enhance the message of the need to preserve the natural environment.

Brother Eagle, Sister Sky. This picture book, by Susan Jeffers, is based on the message Chief Seattle delivered more than a century ago about the need to care about the natural environment.

The values and customs of other cultures, too, often reflect a respect for the natural environment and are sometimes presented in children's books. Following are several such multicultural books.

I Am Eyes/Ni Macho. A beautifully illustrated book by Nonny Hogrogian is about the early morning as seen by a young child in Kenya. Leila Ward is the author.

The Singing Fir Tree. A poetic retelling of a Swiss folktale has special resonance today for people concerned with the preservation of the environment. The retelling of the story is by Barry Root.

Seashore Story. This beautiful picture book and folktale from Japan was done by Taro Yashima.

The Truth About the Moon. In this book by Clayton Bess, an African child is told several stories about the moon, but still feels he has not learned the truth.

Bringing the Rain to Kapiti Plain. This read-along tale by Verna Aardema features appealing rhymes and dramatic folk art illustrating African flora and fauna.

Related Activities

After reading a pro-nature book with the children, share with them your own ideas about why you like the book and what pro-nature themes or ideas were presented in the book. For example, after reading the book, *The Very Hungry Caterpillar*, you might say something like, "Isn't it wonderful how the very hungry caterpillar turned into a beautiful butterfly? It seems like magic." A discussion based on *Home in the Sky* might begin with the statement, "I like the way the story ended with the pigeon flying back to his own home."

In addition to discussing the pro-nature aspects of a book, other follow-up activities might also be introduced. To maintain the children's interest and active involvement, these follow-up activities should ordinarily allow for hands-on experiences. Consider *The House of Leaves*, for example. After reading the story, you might take the children outside to look for the kind of tree Sarah used to protect herself from the rain. Have the children sit quietly under the umbrella of leaves, as Sarah did, and watch for other living creatures who may wish to share the comfort and magic of this house of leaves.

The *Chipmunk Song*, by Joanne Ryder, also lends itself to an outdoor follow-up activity. The text invites readers to imagine that they are living the life of a chipmunk. Children can enter the chipmunk's world by lying on a bed of leaves and imagining themselves sleeping in a cool, dark room under the ground.

In *Anybody Home?*, by Aileen Fisher, a young child finds and wonders about the home of different animals. This story could be followed up with a walk through the school yard in search of animal homes.

> **Related Resources**
>
> *Story Stretchers*, published by Gryphon House. This excellent resource book is written around themes and has suggestions for many of Eric Carle's books, including *The Very Hungry Caterpillar* and *The Very Busy Spider*.
>
> *Keepers of the Earth: Native American Stories and Environmental Activities for Children* (Caduto & Bruchac, 1991) and the teacher's guides that accompanies *Keepers of the Animals* (Caduto & Bruchac, 1991).

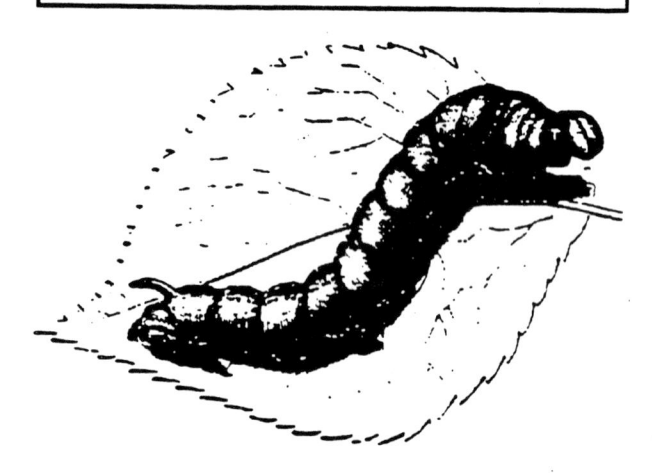

Books and Themes

The idea of themes or units is often used in planning activities over a specified period of time (e.g., week, two-weeks, month, etc,). An appropriate topic is chosen as the theme that then ties activities and experiences together. Typical themes include concepts relating to the weather, community helpers, modes of transportation, seasonal activities, etc.

Children's books are often used to help develop the theme idea. To help children learn more about the natural world, nature-related themes (forests, rocks, oceans, etc.) with corresponding sets of books could be identified.

A unit around the concept of "seeds" might be introduced in Spring. Children could be involved in studying the characteristics of different types of seeds, planting seeds, and preparing snacks with different foods having seeds. The library corner, at this time, could then feature a variety of books on seeds. Presented in Appendix C is a listing of children's books grouped according to topics appropriate for nature-related themes, or units, in an early childhood program.

Poetry and Finger Plays

To help children appreciate nature, you can also introduce nature-related poetry and finger plays. The following references offer many ideas.

Poetry of Earth. (1972). Collected and illustrated by Adrienne Adams. (Available through DLM, One DLM Park, Allen, Texas 75002). This is an anthology of poetry about Earth and its inhabitants. It also includes suggestions for related activities in the classroom. The collection of poems is divided into units for animals, plants, the land, and endangered elements. While it is designed primarily for Grades 2 to 6, some of the poems and activities can be used with younger children.

Picking Up Sunshine. (Available through DLM, One DLM Park, Allen, Texas 75002) This collection of poems is by Leland Jacobs. The book offers suggestions for related activities in the classroom and includes nature-related topics, such as seasons and animals. This book is designed primarily for Grades Pre-K to 3.

Sing a Song of Seasons. (Available through Continental Press, Elizabethtown, PA 17022. Phone: 1-800-233-0759) A collection of seasonal poems for children. Includes poems about gently falling leaves, Jack Frost, Pussy Willows, and other seasonal concepts. In

Big Book format with additional take-home books and a teacher resource guide.

Animals On Parade (Available through Continental Press, Elizabethtown, PA 17022. Phone: 1-800-233-0759) Contents include Puppy, Mice, Eletelephony, The Little Turtle, and The Duckbilled Platypus. In Big Book format with additional take-home books and a teacher resource guide.

Have You Seen Birds? by Joanne Oppenheim and illustrated by Barbara Reid. Presents a lyrical poem about birds. (Available through Scholastic Inc., P.O. Box 7502, Jeffersoan City, MO 65102. Phone: 1-800-631-1586.)

Pumpkin Pumpkin by Jeanne Titherington. Focuses on the wonder of a tiny seed sprout growing into a large pumpkin. (Available through Scholastic Inc., P.O. Box 7502, Jeffersoan City, MO 65102. Phone: 1-800-631-1586.)

Anna's Summer Songs by Mary Q. Stelle with illustrations by Lena Anderson. Anna's joyous songs celebrate trees, flowers, ferns, fruit and everything else that grows. (Available through Scholastic Inc., P.O. Box 7502, Jeffersoan City, MO 6510 2. Phone: 1-800-631-1586.)

Videos

There are some excellent videos, too, that can be used with young children for information on nature . "Bugs Don't Bug Us" is an example of the kind of video that fosters positive attitudes about nature. Through this video, children learn about many of the common invertebrates that share the natural world with us. This video runs approximately 35 minutes and is available from M.S. Creations, P.O. Box 83, Bolivar, MO 65613.

Other Video Resources

The Snowy Day by Ezra Jack Keats. Available through Scholastic (1-800-631-1586).
Seasons by Stonecki. Available through Educational Activities, Inc. Baldwin, NY 11510.

Suggested Children's Books

Martin, Bill, Jr., and John Archambault. *LISTEN TO THE RAIN*. Illustrations by James Endicott. Holt, 1988.Fiction. Interest Level: Ages 3-8.

Recommended Resources

Eyeopeners! How to Choose and Use Children's Books about Real People, Places and Things. B. Kobrin. New York: Penguin Books, 1988.

Science Through Children's Literature. C. Butzow & J. Butzow. Englewood, CO: Teacher's Ideas Press, 1989.

Teaching Kids to Love the Earth. M. Herman, J. Passineau, A. Schimpf, P. Treuer. Duluth, MN: Pfeifer-Hamilton Publishers, 1991.

There Lived a Wicked Dragon. M. Finan, Washington, D.C.: U.S. Environmental Protection Agency, 1973.

Fun With Art
Encouraging Expressions of Wonder

Implementation Guideline # 4: Encourage nature-related art activities.

Nature and art represent a natural combination for fostering the aesthetic development of young children and for helping young children learn about the beauty and diversity inherent in nature. Additionally, materials from nature are abundant and fairly easy to work with.

Because nature has often been used as the subject of art, existing works of art can be used to introduce children to the idea of nature art. Numerous examples of nature art can be found in art museums, books about art, and reproductions for interior decorating. Such reproductions, as well as nature-related posters, can add beauty to the classroom decor and encourage children to get interested in the world of art and nature.

What is most important for fostering the aesthetic development of young children, however, is getting them actively involved in creating their own works of art. Such creations can take many different forms and should often include three-dimensional forms.

Children's works of art should never be judged against some external criteria. Children's works of art are expressions of their own activities and ideas, and should be respected as such. It's good for teachers and parents to focus on the process versus the product. Did the child find beauty and experience joy in the process? If so, the art activity has been successful.

Children's art should be displayed—both at school and at home. A special art show might be arranged—maybe around a special theme (e.g., art reflecting spring, rain, or flowers). Invitations could be made and delivered. Refreshments, a floral arrangement, and soft music could add to the magic of the event. The news media could receive a special invitation, with hopes of getting the art show mentioned in the daily newspaper. Other ways of sharing the joy of children's art is by way of displays at local early childhood conferences, "gifts" to special friends in nursing homes, and individual "Books of Art" as Mother's Day gifts.

You can frame children's works of art using the matting from discarded pictures. You might also hang children's art work over the picture on a calendar.

Following are some ideas on how to involve young children in creating nature art. These ideas represent only a beginning of what might be done. After introducing the idea to children and providing them with a variety of materials, their own creativity is sure to generate many more ways to express their feelings of wonder about the natural world.

Beauty On the Ground and All Around

Background information: This activity involves making a collage from things found in nature. The purpose of the activity is to help children discover beauty in some of the most common aspects of nature—grasses, leaves, seeds, small twigs, etc.

Procedures:
1. Go on an outdoor "beauty hunt." Give each child a small paper bag for collecting materials to use in making a nature collage. Remind the children to take only those things that will not harm the environment. They should avoid picking wildflowers or breaking branches from trees. They may look for seeds, twigs, leaves, dried grass, etc.
2. Sort, compare, and share materials after returning to the classroom.
3. Provide a variety of background materials for the collage and some type of adhesive. Background materials with differing colors should be made available and could include cardboard or flat pieces of bark.

Suggestions:
- Talk about how to choose a background color to best bring out the different colors found in the collage materials.
- Provide a variety of adhesives, including glue, tape, soft clay, string or yarn, etc.

Follow-Up:
Display the children's collages in a special place or for a special occasion. You might also take photos of the children's art and award ribbons for work well done.

Fascinating Shapes

Background information: Collages using a variety of background shapes can help children become more aware of the variety of shapes found in nature.

Procedures:
1. Cut large pieces of heavy paper or cardboard into the shape of something from nature—e.g., a butterfly, leaf, or flower. Provide one such shape for each child.
2. Encourage the children to identify the object from nature represented by the shape of their paper.
3. Cut colorful pictures and shapes from old magazines.
4. Paste the cut-outs on the background paper to make a multi-colored collage.

Suggestions:
- Use small pieces of tissue paper instead of magazine cut-outs.
- Crumble the pieces of paper before attaching them to the background, thus getting a three-dimensional effect.

Follow-up:
- Use these collages to decorate the classroom.

Rubbings From Trees and Other Things

Background information: Rubbings are fairly easy and fun to do. They can help children become more aware of shapes and textures of things in nature.

Procedures:
1. Provide each child with a sheet of heavy paper, a pencil or crayon, and a push pin.
2. Have each child find a tree with something that is of interest to them (e.g., There's a bird nest in its branches. Some of its branches almost touch the ground. It has very large leaves, etc.).
3. Help each child attach their paper to the tree using the push pin.
4. Have the children rub their pencil or crayon gently across the paper a number of times until they see the outline of the bark.

Suggestions:
- Allow children plenty of time to explore different trees before they decide which one they would like to use for their rubbing. Remember: the exploration of the tree is as important as the rubbing!
- Encourage children to work as partners. One child holds the paper while the other child does the rubbing. (This may have to be demonstrated!) The children then exchange roles, so that each child has a chance to do his or her own rubbing.

Follow-up:
- Give the children time to talk about and compare their rubbings. Help them discover likenesses and differences.
- Do follow-up rubbings indoors. Use materials that come from trees: a single leaf, a pattern of small leaves, or the winged seeds from maple trees. Tape these materials to a table top. Cover them with a sheet of paper. It may help to tape the paper to the table as well. The children then rub a crayon or pencil over the paper to bring out the design of the materials underneath. The materials should be fairly flat and the paper somewhat heavy.

Window Hangings

Background information: Lovely window hangings can be made by sealing flower petals, grasses, or fresh leaves between two sheets of waxed paper.

Procedures

1. Cut sheets of wax paper into pieces approximately 4 by 6 inches. Cut enough for each child to have two pieces.
2. Use materials from nature to make a display on one sheet of the wax paper. Use materials that are small and fairly flat (blades of grass, small leaves, flower petals, etc.).
3. Cover the display with a second sheet of wax paper.
4. Use an electric iron or food warming tray to heat and seal the outer edges (frame) of the display. Place a folded newspaper between the wax paper and the heat source to prevent the wax paper from melting on to the heat source.
5. Punch a hole in the middle of one side of the frame.
6. Thread a piece of string or yarn through the hole. Use this as a holder to hang the display by a window.

Suggestions:
- Encourage children to find their own objects from nature. Remind them to take only things that will not harm animals or plants in the natural environment.
- Displays might be built around special themes or concepts. Following are several examples:
  - Things that are green
  - Things that come from a tree (seeds, leaves, small pieces of bark)
  - Things found in a woods
  - Parts of a flower
  - Different kinds of leaves

Follow-up:
- Give the window hangings as gifts for Mother's Day.
- Decorate the classroom with the window hangings.

Fruit and Vegetable Prints

Background Information: Fruits and vegetables come in a wide variety of interesting shapes and textures. While it's important for children to know that food is something to be respected, they can use individual pieces of fresh fruits and vegetables for making interesting prints.

Procedures:
1. Display several different kinds of fruits and vegetables. Choose items that are firm and easy to handle—carrot sticks, apples, peanuts in the shell, potatoes, green peppers, corn on the cob, and oranges.
2. Make a stamp pad by pouring liquid tempera over a folded paper towel in a small tray.
3. Press chosen fruits and vegetables on the stamp pad and then on to a blank sheet of paper.

Suggestion:
- Cut some of the fruits and vegetables. Cut some lengthwise, others crosswise.
- Roll some of the fruits and vegetables across both the ink pad and the paper.

Follow-up:
- After the paint is try, have children identify the prints.

Animal Prints

Background: Children's hands and feet are often used for making prints with paint. The paws of animals can also be used—but only if the animal is not frightened in the process. **Do not use amphibians (frogs, turtles, snakes, worms), as they breathe through their skin and can be harmed if paint clogs their pores.**

Procedures:
1. Place the animal gently on a large stamp pad or pan of tempera paint.
2. Encourage the animal to walk across a sheet of blank paper.
3. Wipe the animal's paws before placing it back in the cage.

Suggestions:
- Before doing this activity, ask the children for their ideas of what would happen if the animal walked through the paint. Encourage them to talk about what the animal prints might look like.

Follow-up:
- Look at pictures of animal tracks in a book. Compare the tracks in the book with the tracks freshly made during this activity.
- Purchase stamps of different kinds of animal tracks. Let the children play with the stamps and stamp pads, making their own trails across sheets of paper. You might encourage "story telling" while they make their tracks. "Story telling" involves making up stories about what the animal might be doing or where it's going. To enhance this activity, bushes, trees, tunnels etc. might be drawn on the paper. Animal tracks can then be made going to and from the places drawn on the paper.

Mobiles

Background information: Mobiles can be made from real objects found in nature (pine cones, twigs, etc.), pictures or representations of things in nature, or a combination of the two.

Procedures:
1. Find a small tree branch that could serve as the hanger for the mobile. Avoid breaking a branch from a tree. Either use one that is already on the ground or one that needs to be pruned from a tree.
2. Cut shapes of leaves, butterflies, stars, or flowers from colored paper.
3. Punch a hole in each of the shapes.
4. Thread a piece of yarn or string through the hole and tie it to the branch.
5. Also tie pine cones, shells, dried grasses, evergreen sprigs, and other real objects from nature to the mobile.
6. Hang the mobile from the ceiling.

Suggestions:
- Use decorated branches for a bulletin board display. Decorate with the following:
    - children's drawing of early spring leaves or colored fall leaves
    - children's drawings of birds or pictures of birds cut from magazines
    - small kites
    - tissue paper blossoms
    - strips of cotton to represent snow
- Keep one fairly-large branch in the room throughout the year. Decorate to match the different seasons.

Follow-up:
- Take photos of children around the mobile or decorated branch. Have children dressed to match the season—coats and hats for winter, shorts for summer, rain gear for spring, and light jackets for Fall. Make a year-end display featuring the photos from the different seasons.

Real and Pretend Photos

Background information: A camera and the outdoors make an excellent combination for fostering an aesthetic appreciation of nature. For young children, a Polaroid camera is often nice, in that they get instant results. Other types of cameras (including "pretend" cameras) can also be used with very satisfying results.

Procedures:
1. Collect small thin boxes (e.g., glove boxes or blank check boxes) for making "pretend" cameras.
2. Cut a "window" through the boxes to help the children focus on the pictures they want to take.
3. Go outdoors and "take pictures" of favorite things.

Suggestions:
- Display nature posters on the walls of the classroom.
- Use pictures from magazines and old postcards to make a picture album of things found in nature.
- Develop a set of picture cards (the size of playing cards) displaying things from nature. Laminate the cards and encourage matching and sorting activities.
- Take photos of outdoor places in or near the school yard. Take the photos outdoors to the spots where they were taken and look for changes in the environment since the time of the photo session.

Follow-up:
- Incorporate photos into experience stories. Display these stories for parents and visitors to enjoy.

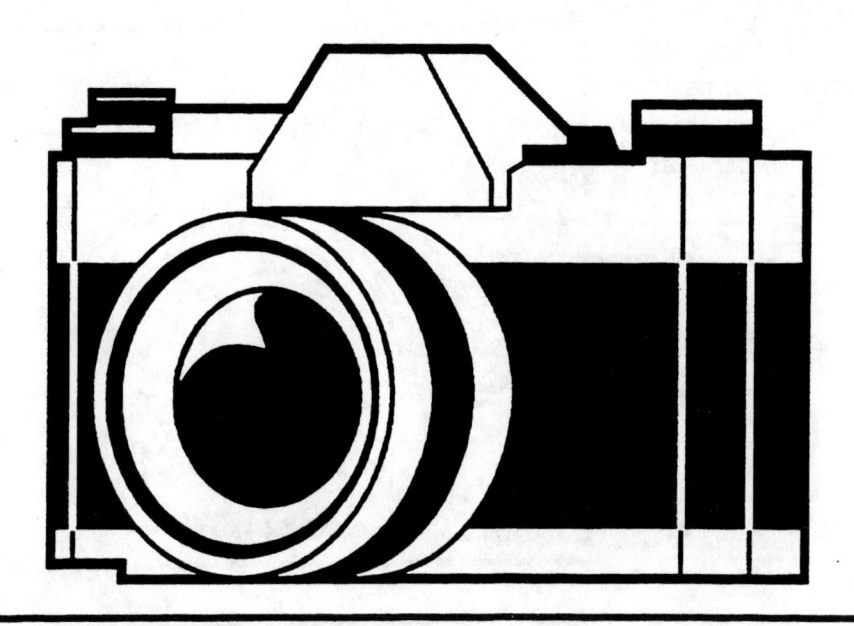

Painting with Nature's Colors

Background information: Grass, dandelion blossoms, and orange peels can be used for painting with materials from nature—so can green leaves and carrot sticks. There are other materials from nature that work as well, including soft stones and clay from the earth.

Procedures:
1. Choose one thing from nature that you can use for "painting." Use it to make an abstract picture or design.
2. Encourage the children to think of other things from nature that might be used for painting.
3. Go outside and collect things that could possibly be used for painting. Avoid picking wildflowers (other than dandelions!).
4. Provide sheets of blank paper for children to experiment with the objects they found. Do the objects work for painting? Which objects work the best? Why do some objects work better than others?

Suggestions:
- Allow plenty of time for experimentation and discussion.
- Rub plant material between your fingers for a minute or two to bring the juice and the pigment to the surface.
- Introduce the concept of using objects from nature to "color in" the picture of something from nature. (Example: A soft green leaf might be used to color in a line drawing of a frog.)

Follow-up:
- Display the children's pictures with an explanation of what objects were used for painting. The actual objects might even be displayed along with the pictures.

Artistic Arrangements

Background information: Using flowers and other materials from nature to make a decorative arrangement can be a rewarding experience and help children grow in appreciation of the beauty of nature.

Procedures:
1. Go outdoors and collect small items of various sizes, colors, and shapes. While collecting these materials talk about and model caring for the natural environment. Materials lending themselves well to this activity include small twigs, leaves, pebbles, pine cones, shells, seeds and nuts.
2. Provide materials on which (or in which) artistic arrangements can be made. These could include baskets, pieces of bark, vases, cans, bottles, pieces of colorful cloth, and shoe box lids.
3. Provide materials that could be used for holding materials in place. Clay works well for a base. Tape, glue, and yarn can be used for holding different materials together. (Children may need a helping hand in holding things together or tying knots.)
4. Encourage the children to use their creativity in making artistic arrangements.

Suggestions:
- Add children's drawings or cut out shapes to decorate the background area.
- Use the entire sandtable for making a collaborative nature art exhibit. Use a collection of twigs, pine cones, dried grasses, leaves, and pods to create small landscapes in the sand. Add toy animals and people figurines, if you wish. If the sandtable is not available, use a large ceramic bowl or shallow plastic tub.

Follow-up:
- Designate a section of the room as an art gallery for displaying children's work. Also use sections of the school library, cafeteria, or entry area for displaying children's work. Label each child's work with his or her name.
- Take pictures of the art gallery and the individual arrangements. Share these pictures with parents.
- Make a video tape of each artist showing and telling something about his or her own work.

Nature Boxes*

Background information: Nature boxes are fun because they provide a vehicle for children to make a picture come alive.

Procedure
1. Collect the necessary materials: shoe boxes, old magazines with pictures of nature, scissors, and glue.
2. Help the children line the shoe boxes with scenes cut from old magazines.
3. Cut narrow strips of cardboard (about one inch by six inches). Cut two or three for each shoebox.
4. Cut two or three slits (large enough to insert the cardboard strips) in the sides of the shoe box.
5. Insert the cardboard strips.
6. Find and cut out small objects of things from nature (sun, animals trees, etc.).
7. Affix the small cut outs to one end of the cardboard strip (the end inside the box).
8. Children move the other end to make movement in the scene.

Suggestions:
- Plan this project far enough in advance to get parents involved in saving shoe boxes and old magazines.
- Encourage children to make up stories about what's happening in their nature scenes.

Follow-up:
- Encourage children to share their boxes with one another, so that each child gets to play with a variety of nature boxes.

Recommended Resources

Good Earth Art: Environmental Art for Kids. M. Kohl & C. Gainer. Bellingham, WA: Bright Ring Publishing, 1991.

Beautiful Junk: Creative Classroom Uses for Recyclable Materials. K. Brackett & R. Manley. Carthage IL: Fearon Teacher Aids, 1990.

---

* This activity submitted by Justine Magsig, as remembered from childhood.

Music and Movement

Implementation Guideline #5: Introduce nature-related music and movement activities.

The world of nature is full of music and movement. The wind in the trees, the sound of crashing waves, and the patter of rain drops are among the natural sounds which surround us. Such sounds can affect our mood, excite our curiosity, and delight our sense of hearing. Listening to such sounds can also help us learn about the world around us.

Movement is a natural accompaniment to music. The pairing of music and movement can be as expressive and spontaneous as a bird or butterfly in flight or as rhythmic and repetitious as the sound of waves along the beach.

Both spontaneous and structured music activities can enhance a child's awareness of music and movement. Such activities can also foster body awareness, motor development, and socialization. The opportunities for imitation and repetition through music and movement activities tend to enhance cognitive and language development as well. Such activities can also heighten the child's interest in the world of nature.

Music and movement activities can take many different forms— from listening to music and participating in sing-a-longs and finger plays, to expressing oneself through pantomimes, dancing, and marching. Music and movement activities should always be fun for the children and provide opportunities for self-expression.

There are numerous ways in which the world of nature might be linked to a variety of music and movement activities. Following are several suggestions.

Sound Recordings From Nature

Background information: Really hearing and appreciating the sounds of nature may take practice. Hearing some of the softer sounds requires careful attention. Children may need some help in learning to listen for the sounds of nature in their environment.

Procedures:
1. Introduce children to the tape recording function of a tape recorder. As an introduction, you may wish to have each child talk into the microphone, with a statement such as "Hi, my name is _____." After each child records his or her own statement, rewind and playback the messages.
2. Invite individual children to record additional statements, **without giving their names**. You may suggest "starters" such as, "My favorite food is _____," or "My favorite color is _____." As these statements are played back, children are asked to identify the speakers, by the sounds of their voices and by what they said.
3. You, the tape recorder, and the children go outdoors. Ask the children to listen for sounds of nature (i.e., sounds coming from plants, animals, wind, running water, etc.). Talk with the children about which sounds they would like to record, and then make tape recordings based on their suggestions.

Suggestions:
- Before going outside with the children to tape record sounds of nature, identify for yourself areas that are most conducive to this activity. You might look for a wooded area where the children are likely to hear the sound of wind in the trees, birds singing, and squirrels or chipmunks rustling in the leaves. You might also look for a stream, bees buzzing around flowers, and branches of trees rubbing against each other. Sometimes in the fall, you can hear leaves blowing across the yard; and in the late summer, the sound of cicadas filling the air. For this activity, it's also important to use a fairly good tape recorder and to ask the children to be very quiet while taping the sounds of nature. Try to avoid areas polluted by the sound of traffic and other people-made noises.

Follow-up:
- After returning to the classroom, ask the children to listen to and identify the recorded sounds of nature. You might also ask them to recall the place where the sounds were heard.
- Add the "sounds of nature" tape to the children's listening library for individual use. Also, make the tape

Part II: Implementing the Curriculum

available for "check out" so that children might share the tape with their parents and siblings. A newsletter and/or photo album might accompany the tape, to help family members recognize the source of the recorded sounds.
- Find a pre-recorded tape of nature sounds.* Ask the children to sit or lie quietly while they listen to the tape. Ask them to listen carefully for sounds of nature, because after the listening session you will be asking them to identify the sounds they heard. After a few minutes of listening time, have the children share ideas about the sounds they heard.
- Play tapes of nature sounds at nap or rest time to help children relax.
- Give each child a large sheet of drawing paper and one or two crayons. Have the children freely draw lines and swirls while listening to a pre-recorded tape of nature sounds. Invite the children to talk about the "pictures" they made and the feelings they had while listening to the tape. Write captions on the pictures, labeling some of the sounds the children heard (e.g., water falling, wind blowing, etc.). For this activity, you may choose to let the children discover the presence of nature sounds in the music, versus telling them ahead of time that they will be hearing sounds of nature on the tape.
- Use a pre-recorded tape of nature sounds as background music while children are engaged in free play activities, while they rest, or have a snack.

---

* Pre-recorded tapes with sounds of nature are available through many bookstores, gift shops, and even some health food stores. Some such tapes combine instrumental music with sounds of nature. These tapes are especially nice for background music and "drawing-to-music" activities.

Listen to Music about Nature

Background information: Pre-recorded sounds of nature can be used to help children become more aware and appreciative of the beauty and diversity of sounds in the natural world.

Procedures.
1. Collect some pre-recorded records and/or tapes with songs about nature. Get acquainted with these songs.
2. Collect some "props" (e.g., pictures, stuffed animals, etc.) relating to the songs.
3. Share the music and the props with the children. Encourage them to be good listeners so that they can learn the words to the songs.
4. Introduce simple body movements to go along with the children's favorite songs. Invite children to share their ideas on what movements might go well with the music.
5. Listen and move to the music.

Suggestions:
- Share the lyrics of children's favorite songs with the parents. This might be done by way of a parent newsletter and/or making the audiotapes available on a check-out basis.

Follow-up:
- Encourage children to use the records and tapes on their own during "free play" or "center time." They may wish to listen individually (by way of headphones) or in small groups. Provide accompanying props, and encourage related body movements and drawings.

Recommended Resources

Earthy Tunes. (audiocassette) M. Miche. Berkeley, CA: Song Trek Music

The Frog Chorus: Songs, Stories, and Activities. (audiocassette) D. Stokes. Milwaukee, WI: Schlitz Audobon Center, 1991.

Part II: Implementing the Curriculum

Recommended Resources

Nature Songs for Children

TITLE/ARTIST	PUBLISHER/CONTACT
Birds (Hap Palmer)	Educational Activities, Inc. Freeport, N.Y. 11520
Animal Antics (Hap Palmer)	Educational Activities, Inc. Freeport, N.Y. 11520
Turtles & Snakes & Snowstorms (Axelrod, G.)	Folkways Records 43 W. 61st St. New York, NT 10023
You'll Sing a Song (Jenkins, E.)	(212) 777-6606
Songs & Stories for Children (Gentle Wind)	Gentle Wind Box 3103 Albany, NT 12203 (518) 482-9023
Magical Place (Clement, R.)	Tomorrow River Music Box 165 Madison, WI 53701
Billy B Sings About Trees (Brennan, B.)	Annie Tiberio 62 Mountain Road Hampden, MA 01036
Romp in the Swamp (Brennan, B.)	(413) 566-8980
Spin, Spider, Spin (Brennan, B.)	Educational Activities, Inc. Baldwin, NY 11510
Piggyback Planet (Rogers, S.)	Round River Records E. Lansing, MI
Grandpa Art's Nature	Cimino Publishing, 1-800-227-2712
Songs for Children (Custer, A.)	Scholastic, 1-800-631-1586
Animal Piggyback Songs	Redleaf Press, 1-800-423-8309
Ever Green, Ever Blue (Raffi)	MCA Records, Universal City, CA

63

Nature's Musical Instruments

Background information: A variety of musical instruments can be made from objects found in nature; others can be purchased. Using such instruments can provide a musical delight and foster an appreciation of the beauty and wonder of nature.

Procedures:
1. Display a variety of musical instruments and pictures of musical instruments. Talk about what the instruments are made from (e.g., guitar made from wood, drum made from animal skin, etc.).
2. Collect objects of nature that could be used for making musical instruments. These could include sea shells, a small hollow log, dried gourds, seeds or kernels of corn (to be used with baby food jars or film canisters to make maracas), a pine sprig (to make a swishing sound when brushed over a drum), and a pair of sticks (to rub or tap together). Invite the children's ideas on what else from nature could be used in making musical instruments.
3. Work with the children in constructing musical instruments.
4. Invite children to play their instrument of choice. Encourage turn taking for conducting the band; also encourage turn taking for sitting in the audience. Have the band play along with a record or tape.

Suggestions:
- Tell the parents in advance about this project. Invite them to visit the class and share any instrument they may play. Encourage them to talk about the instrument and how it's made, as well as performing for the children. Also invite their ideas and contributions for making instruments from objects of nature.

Follow-up:
- Put on a band performance for the parents or other classes in the school. Videotape the event and play it back for the children to enjoy.

Imitate Animals

Background information: Children can grow in understanding and appreciation of animals by studying the way they move. Because young children learn by doing, observing and then imitating animals is a developmentally appropriate way of learning about animal behavior.

Procedures:
1. Encourage children to think about the way different animals move. You might give some simple examples, using props and demonstrations, as appropriate. Then have the children individually demonstrate the movements of an animal with which they are somewhat familiar.
2. Have the children watch each other doing animal imitations. Have them guess which animal is being imitated.

Suggestions:
- Introduce pictures, books, and videos about animals to help children learn about how animals move. Public television and the Discovery Channel frequently feature programs about animals.
- Introduce short videos of dances by ethnic groups (Native Americans, Mexicans, etc.) that include moving like animals.

Follow-up:
- Introduce an animal form of the game, "Simon Says". To play this game, children are asked to space themselves throughout the room so that they each child has enough space for active movements. Children are to listen carefully to the leader who calls for some type of "animal-imitation movement" (e.g., "fly like a bird" or "crawl like a worm"). Children are to execute the movement only if the leader begins a directive with the words "Simon Says." If the leader does not say "Simon Says," players are to stand in place without moving. Following are some examples of "animal-imitation movements" that might be used. Be sure to include the children's ideas and give them a turn to serve as leader.
  - peck like a woodpecker
  - stretch your neck like a giraffe
  - curl up like a caterpillar
  - fly like a butterfly
  - walk like a duck
  - chew like a squirrel
  - wiggle your nose like a rabbit
  - drink like a chicken

Nature Charades

Background information: After children learn about the life cycles and characteristic behaviors of several different plants and animals, a simple game of "nature charades" can be introduced.

Procedures:
1. Demonstrate one or two examples of motions illustrating animal behavior or other phenomena in nature. Talk the movements through with the children as you do so. Following are several examples of movements you might use.
    - Grow from a seed to a flower. Curl up on the floor pretending to be seeds in the ground. Stretch your arms and legs like roots seeking water. Get up slowly, as a stem reaching for the sunlight. Make leaf-like shapes with your hands. Stretch your neck upwards and turn your face toward the sky. Your face is the flower that now blooms in the sunshine. Move your head and the rest of your body to imitate a swaying in the breeze.
    - Grow from a caterpillar to a butterfly.
    - Change from a tadpole into a frog.
    - Be a bird and go through the nest-building process.
    - Be a turtle and hide your head inside your shell.
2. Invite individual children to act the motions of a plant or animal, without using words. The other children are to guess what is being demonstrated.

Suggestions:
- Display pictures illustrating different phenomena in nature.

Follow-Up:
- Make play-dough representations of different phenomena in nature.
- Provide stuffed animals, animal figurines, or animal puppets and appropriate props to act out animal behaviors. One example is to use a toy bird. Provide nesting material, plastic eggs, and pretend bird seed.

Enjoying the Seasons

Implementation Guideline # 6: Celebrate each of the seasons with special nature-related activities

Observing changes in the natural environment from one season to the next can help young children become better observers of nature and spark their interest in the world around them. Changes throughout the different seasons can be studied, using a scientific approach. Such changes can also be celebrated, using a more affective approach. While both approaches can be incorporated appropriately into an early childhood program, focusing on the affective dimensions can provide an excellent vehicle for the aesthetic development of young children—an area of development that is often slighted in favor of cognitive and pre-academic concerns. There are ways to integrate the scientific and affective approaches to learning about the different seasons and it is this integrated approach that is supported by the following suggested activities.

Fall Celebrations

Fall can be celebrated and enjoyed in a variety of ways by using items that are plentiful during this season of the year. Such items include apples, pumpkins, and leaves.

Apple activities:
- Pick them.
- Wash them.
- Peel and slice them.
- Make apple sauce and apple butter
- Eat them with peanut butter.
- Eat them with cheese and crackers.
- Describe them and count them.
- Read books about apples.
- Color paper apples and attach them to an apple tree mural.
- Stuff small red cloth bags with crumpled newspaper to make three dimensional apples.
- Compare apples to pears and oranges. How do they look, feel, smell, and taste different?

Pumpkin activities:
- Paint faces on pumpkins.
- Cut them open to discover what's inside.
- Pound nails into them.
- Use them for room decorations.
- Wash and roast the pumpkin seeds.
- Plant a few pumpkin seeds in large indoor containers.
- Make pumpkin pie or pumpkin pudding

Leaf activities:
- Rake them.
- Roll and jump in then.
- Stuff them in bags. Hide behind the bags.
- Add them to a compost pile.
- Make leaf prints and leaf collages.
- Spray paint around them.
- Press them and laminate them.
- Sort them according to size, shape, or color.
- Order them from smallest to largest.
- Use them for room decorations.

Halloween Fun

Background information: Next to Thanksgiving, Halloween is probably the most popular holiday of the fall season. There are several fun-filled ways to introduce nature appreciation concepts into the Halloween celebrations, including having children dress up as plants or animals. The process of designing and making animal or plant costumes will provide many opportunities for introducing some interesting facts about the plants or animals the children wish to represent.

Procedures:
1. Invite the children's ideas as to what plant or animal they would like to be.
2. Plan a simple way as to how the desired plants and animals might be represented. You may wish to focus on only one aspect of the plant or animal—e.g., a tiger's tail, the petals of a sunflower, the wings of a butterfly, etc.
3. Gather the necessary materials.
4. Make the costumes, involving the children's help as much as possible.
5. March in parade.

Suggestions:
- Plan a parent/child work-session at school for making the costumes. Have available the materials and ideas on how to make different costumes. Ask the parents for ideas, as well.
- Take lots of pictures.
- Videotape the process of making the costumes as well as the parade. You may wish to videotape steps throughout the entire process—from the choosing of what animal or plant to be, to wearing the costume and pretending to be that animal or plant.

Follow-up:
- Write an experience story of the process.
- Discuss habitats for the different animal characters. Talk about where the animals live and what they eat. Have children role play the life of the animal in its habitat.

Enjoying the Harvest

Background information: Fall is a wonderful time of the year to visit orchards, farms, and gardens. Many fruits and vegetables are being harvested, and the process, if explained in simple terms, can be fascinating to young children.

Procedures:
1. Visit a "farmers' market" or roadside stand.
2. Involve children in choosing which fruits and vegetables to purchase for snack or lunch.
3. Involve children in cleaning and preparing the fruits and vegetables for snack or lunch.
4. Enjoy the food!

Suggestions:
- Visit a field, garden, or orchard where the fruit and vegetables grow.
- Talk about the differences between growing under the ground or on a tree or bush.

Follow-up:
- Provide the necessary props for a "pretend" road-side stand in the classroom.

Suggested Children's Books

Autumn Story by Jill Barklem
Autumn Harvest by Alvin Tresselt
Autumn by Lucille Wood
Apple Tree by P. Parnell
Autumn Story by Jill Barklem

Winter Activities

Winter is not a time to hibernate indoors and wait for better weather in order to do interesting nature-related activities. The following suggestions are designed to get you thinking about the variety of nature-related activities you can do to celebrate and enjoy the winter season.

Making Christmas/Winter Decorations

Background information: One way to bring nature indoors in the winter time is to use materials from nature to make lovely classroom decorations.

Procedures:
1. Gather the following materials: a variety of small evergreen sprigs, one or more ring mold pans, ribbon, miniature Christmas tree decorations, pinecones, and a string of popcorn.
2. Fill the ring mold about three-fourths full with water.
3. Float several evergreen sprigs on the water.
4. Add pieces of ribbon, Christmas tree decorations, pinecones, and popcorn string.
5. Enjoy the wreath!

Suggestions:
- Display pictures of wreaths.
- Display pictures of evergreen trees.

Follow-up:
- Send directions for this activity home to the parents.
- Have children sponge paint on wreath-shaped paper.
- Have children paint with small evergreen sprigs.

Grow Your Own Icicle

Background information: Timing is important, as this activity will work only when the temperature is at freezing or below.

Procedures:
1. Puncture a small hole in the bottom of a plastic bottle (one way to recycle a 2-liter pop bottle!).
2. Partially fill the bottle with water.
3. Tie the bottle to a low-hanging tree branch or other structure outdoors.
4. Check it the next day to see if an icicle has grown.

Suggestions:
- Before doing this activity, ask the children what they think will happen when the bottle is put outside.
- Hang two bottles outside—one in a sunny area, the other in a shady area. Watch for differences.

Follow-up:
- Once the icicle forms, take the bottle indoors. Watch as the ice turns back to water.
- Add the bottle to the water table. Let the children enjoy filling the bottle and watching the water leak. Keeping the bottle around after the "experiment" stimulates further discussion of what happened.

Part II: Implementing the Curriculum

Fun in the Snow

Background information: Snow is too wonderful to stay indoors on a snowy day. Go outdoors and encourage free play and exploration.

Procedures:
1. Bundle up in warm clothes. Everyone must wear boots.
2. Explore different areas of the school yard. Note which areas of the yard have the deepest snow. Encourage the children to talk about why the snow is deeper in some areas than in others.

Suggestions:
- Talk to parents in advance about the importance of warm clothes and boots for their children. Encourage the parents to provide boots that are easy to get off and on.
- Have an extra supply of gloves, scarves, and boots for children who may not have any.
- While outside, go on a discovery hunt. Can you find any signs of animals, such as tracks in the snow?

Follow-up:
- After returning to the classroom, have the children share their experiences and ideas about the snow. Write down what they say. Share this with the parents.
- Fill the water table or buckets with snow. Encourage the children to play with and make observations about the snow when it's indoors.

Paper Snowflakes

Background information:
Snowflakes are marvelous sources of beauty and wonder. Children who have first-hand experience of snow as well as those who live in areas where it never snows will enjoy learning about the wonder of snowflakes. One way to learn about snow is to make paper snowflakes.

Procedures:
1. Select easy-to-fold white paper.
2. Draw a circle on the paper (about the size of a small paper plate).
3. Cut out the circle.
4. Fold the circle in half and then the half-circle into thirds.
5. Make cuts anywhere on any side of the folded paper.
6. Unfold your six-sided snowflake.

Suggestions:
- Prepare the materials in advance. For some children, this may mean having everything complete except unfolding the paper that is already cut.
- To make the snowflakes sparkle, "wet" the snowflake with diluted glue and then sprinkle with salt or glitter. This works well for snowflakes displayed on a flat surface, but may cause hanging snowflakes to fold and sag.

Follow-up:
- Use the snowflakes to decorate the classroom. Hang them in the windows and from the ceiling. Hang them on an evergreen branch brought into the classroom.

Capture Real Snowflakes

Background information:
Snowflakes are beautiful but elusive. They can be captured, however, and observed close up.

Procedures:
1. Get a small piece of glass, a piece of cardboard, a small bowl, and some hair spray.
2. Put the glass and the hair spray in the freezer or outside so that they'll become as cold as the outside air.
3. When it's snowing and you're ready to catch a snowflake, put the glass on a piece of cardboard. Use some type of sticky putty to hold the glass in place.
4. Grasp the piece of cardboard—not the glass, so your hands won't warm the glass.
5. Spray the glass with a thick layer of hair spray.
6. Hold the glass out in the snow until you've caught a few flakes.
7. Cover the glass and the snowflakes with the bowl. Leave it outside to dry for about an hour.
8. Take the preserved snowflakes indoors and study them more closely with a magnifying glass.

Suggestions:
- Because of the multi-step process involved in this activity, you may wish to work with only a small group of children at a time. Have enough materials available to repeat this activity several times.

Follow-up:
- Encourage snow-flake drawings after children have experienced this activity.
- Show other nature items (or pictures of items) that have star or snowflake shapes (e.g., center of an apple cut crosswise, the flower of a violet or shooting star).

Sprout Plants Indoors

Background information: Winter is a wonderful time to enjoy flowers indoors. Tulips, hyacinths, and daffodils sprout well indoors. Bulbs and directions on how to grow them indoors can usually be obtained from a garden store. Hyacinth bulbs will sprout and grow in water as well as in soil. For sprouting in water, follow these steps:

Procedures:
1. Fill a jar about four-fifths full of water.
2. Set a hyacinth bulb in the water. You want only the bottom of the bulb submerged. You may need to hold the bulb up with sturdy toothpicks stuck into the sides of the bulb. Use a clear glass jar so that the children can see the roots developing.

Suggestions:
- In the late winter or early spring, force leaves on tree and shrub branches to open indoors. Willows work well; so do forsythia, crab apple, and flowering plums. Wait until the trees have budded, then carefully cut a small branch slantways with a sharp knife. Bring it indoors and put it in a glass of warm water. Place this near a sunny window and watch the buds swell and break open.
- Display pictures of flowering plants.
- Provide books with pictures of flowers in bloom.

Follow-up:
- Encourage children to draw or paint pictures, using colors that match the flowers.
- Use a magnifying glass to study more closely the different parts of the flower.

Spring Celebrations

Spring is a great time of the year to enjoy and celebrate the world of nature. Following are several spring activities appropriate for a group of preschool children.

Multisensory Springtime Walk

Background information: "Looking for signs of spring" is a common focus for a springtime walk. While such a focus may be fun and interesting, it may come up somewhat short in engaging all the senses and thus limiting one's enjoyment of nature. A multisensory springtime walk may be a delightful alternative. The following pre-trip activities might be used to sharpen sensory awareness.

Procedures—Pre-trip activities:

1. Sharpen the sense of hearing. Engage the children in listening to heartbeats through a stethoscope. Have them listen to their own heartbeat, their friend's, and the classroom pet's. Encourage them to listen for differences in their heartbeat and the heartbeat of the rabbit or guinea pig. Later, when the children go outdoors, encourage them to listen for the "heartbeat" of a tree and the "heartbeat" of the earth. They (and you!) may be surprised as to what you hear. The sense of hearing can also be heightened by listening to and joining in on the repetitive sounds in such children's books as *Over in the Meadow* by Ezra Jack Keats.

    Another listening activity involves having children close their eyes and then listening for either environmental sounds or sounds made by the teacher (e.g. tapping a pencil, ringing a bell, etc.). Children can sit or lie on the floor with their eyes closed. They are asked to point in the direction from where the sound is coming. Individual children can be called on to identify the source of the sound (i.e., what made the sound you heard?).

2. Sharpen the sense of sight. Challenge the children to carefully attend to different colors and shapes. Bring in a variety of objects from nature. These could include seeds, pine cones, leaves, twigs, etc. Lay out on a table blocks, or drawings, of different shapes (square, triangle, circle). Ask the children to look carefully at the items from nature and match them with the different shapes. If they need help in getting started, you might show them how the end of a small branch is often shaped like a circle, and that many pine cones have a triangular shape.

3. Sharpen the sense of smell. Provide a variety of materials with pleasant, distinctive scents.

Include items from nature such as a cupful of damp earth, freshly cut wood, crushed leaves, bags of herbal tea, and fresh flowers.
4. Sharpen the sense of taste. Introduce a wide variety of raw fruits and vegetables—both separately and in combination. These could include cucumbers, green peppers, raw potatoes, grapefruit slices, kiwi fruit, blueberries, cabbage, and other foods which may be new to some of the children.

    Have children compare the taste of one piece of fruit to another one of its kind. You might choose an apple or an orange. Give each child his or her own pre-sliced piece of fruit. Ask the children to taste just one slice at first and eat it very slowly. Encourage them to pay close attention to how it tastes. Is it sweet; very sweet; a little sour; etc? Then ask them to exchange a slice of their fruit with a slice of fruit from a child sitting next to them. Does this slice taste a little different? Is it sweeter, a little more sour, etc.?
5. Sharpen the sense of touch. Use snack time to introduce a variety of textures as well as tastes. Encourage children to feel with their fingers and their tongues the textures of the different foods. How does a cracker feel in comparison to bread? How does the inside of the apple feel in comparison to the outside? How about the inside and outside of a banana? And doesn't a spoonful of ice cream feel wonderful when first placed in your mouth?

Procedures—Outdoor activities:
1. Encourage children to see, feel, and smell the new green plants and small wildflowers.
2. Call attention to the singing of birds and the croaking of frogs.
3. Have the children feel the softness of grass and the dampness of earth.

Suggestions:
- Encourage the children to add their ideas as to how they might experience the wonders of spring.

Follow-up:
- Encourage children to role play what it's like to work outside in the spring. Provide child-sized gardening tools and a tub of dirt.
- Encourage children to draw or paint pictures of what they experienced outdoors. Provide photos or pictures of clouds, trees, grass, birds, and flowers to encourage children's artistic expressions. Have plenty of paper, crayons, paint, etc. available for their use.
- Provide stencils or templates featuring the shapes of certain springtime phenomena (e.g., flowers, butterflies, and birds).
- Read stories and provide picture books relating to spring and springtime activities.

Suggested Children's Books

Springtime Walk by Lucille Wood

Springfellow by Robert Kraus.

Sprouting Beans

Background information: Seeds play an important role in the spring of the year. Activities to help children learn more about seeds can range from observing seeds to watching them grow.

Procedures:
1. Give each child a dried bean. Lima beans and navy beans work well.
2. Tell the children that the bean is a type of seed and that there's something special inside every seed. Encourage them to find out what's special about the seed.
3. Children will discover that the "special part" is a tiny new plant growing inside the seed.
4. Provide a magnifying glass for closer inspection.
5. Give each child a plastic sandwich bag, a dampened white paper towel, and a two or three beans.
6. Help the children fold the paper towel and place it in the bag.
7. Place the beans between the paper toweling and the side of the bag.
8. Provide help in stapling the bags shut and labeling them with each child's name. Masking tape works well for name labels.
9. Place the sprouting bags in an area where they're protected from direct sunlight and from too much handling.
10. Look at the bags every day to watch for newly sprouted beans.

Suggestions:
- Tell the parents in advance about this project. Let them know that you will be sending the bean sprouts home. Suggest that they prepare a place in the yard or garden to plant the seedlings.

Follow-up:
- Write an experience story about the bean seeds. Include appropriate drawings to show the growth of the seedlings.

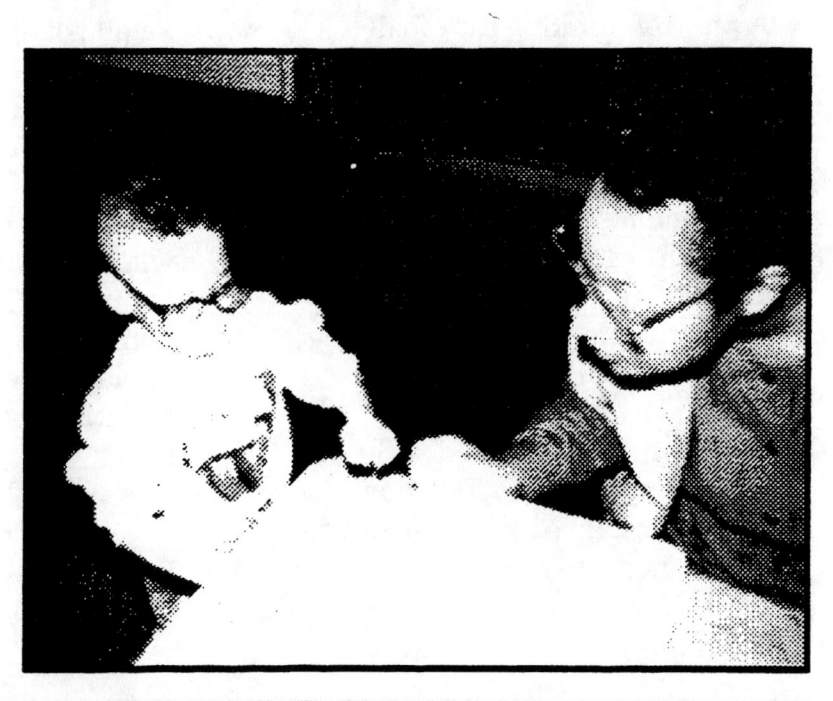

Growing Flowers

Background information: Children learn about the magic of seeds when they're given the opportunity to grow their own flowers from seeds. Marigolds and zinnias work well for this activity.

Procedures:
1. Cut cardboard egg cartons apart to make separate cups.
2. Fill the "cups" almost to the top with soil. (Commercial potting soil is best, as it is sterilized.)
3. Place the filled cup in an intact egg carton (one that is not cut apart), to prevent the cup from tipping.
4. Use a medicine dropper or very small bottle to dampen the soil.
5. Place a flower seed on top of the soil. Cover it with a spoonful of soil. Press gently and water again.
6. Label each cup with a child's name. A piece of masking tape folded against itself and attached to a toothpick might be used for making the name tags.
7. Slide the egg cartons into plastic bags and fasten with a twister.
8. Store the egg cartons away from direct sunlight and other heat.
9. Water the plants every day using the medicine dropper or small bottle to avoid over watering.
10. Keep the plants covered with the plastic bag until the first small leaves appear. At this time, cover only at night to retain moisture.
11. After the second pair of leaves appear, give the seedlings a few hours of direct sunlight everyday. This can be done outdoors in a sheltered spot.

Suggestions:
- Send the seedlings home with the children. Prepare them for a safe trip home by placing the cups in small milk cartons stuffed with crumpled paper. Write a note to the parents with suggestions for transplanting the seedlings.
- The seedlings can be transplanted into a small container (one that holds about three cups of soil) before the children take them home. If put into flower pots and decorated with a ribbon, these make nice Mother's Day gifts. When transplanting into a small pot, first put a layer of small stones and then fill with soil.
- For additional planting experience, order seedlings from the county Soil and Water Conservation office. Seedlings are usually provided without cost. It's best to order in January or February for a Spring planting. Arrangements can be made to plant the seedlings at home, school, or with permission in a nearby park.

Follow-up:
- Encourage the children to act out the process of growing from a seed into a flowering plant. One or several children can start by curling up on the floor. Other children water the seeds. Some one is the sun and shines on the seeds. The seeds begin to grow. A flower blooms.

- Encourage children to talk about what it might feel like to be a seed in the ground or a flower blooming in the sun.

Letter to Parents

Dear Parents,
   On (date), we planted marigold (or zinnia) seeds. We watered our plants everyday. We watched them grow and get some leaves. If the ground is warm, the plant is ready to grow outdoors. Please plant in a somewhat sunny area
   The plant could also be put in a flower pot. Please add some small stones first and use a container that is big enough to hold about three cups of soil.
   We hope that the plant grows for you and that you enjoy this gift!

Celebrate the Coming of Spring

Background information: Because of the special beauty and wonder of nature during spring, the beginning of this season calls for a real celebration. A "Let's Celebrate Spring" party is sure to receive the enthusiastic support of parents and the community.

Procedures:
1. Set the date as close to the first day of Spring as possible.
2. Prepare and deliver (or mail) invitations. Be sure to invite the parents.
3. Plan the details of the party, including decorations, a special visitor or video, refreshments, and outdoor fun.
4. Throw the party and have a wonderful time.

Suggestions:
- Contact a nursery or greenhouse for a donation of flowers.
- Ask the owner of a toy store or hobby shop to donate a kite.
- Make or purchase pinwheels—one for each child
- Assemble materials for blowing bubbles in the wind. The plastic rings used on 6-pack beverages are great for making soap bubbles. Children dip the plastic rings in a container of soap solution and then wave them gently in the wind. This works well for making bubbles and is an excellent way to recycle the plastic. Discard the rings appropriately when no longer usable.

Follow-up:
- Write thank you notes to all who contributed to the springtime party. Decorate with children's drawings of flowers.

Summer Celebrations

The opportunities for outdoor summer play and learning about nature are endless. Following is just one suggestion.

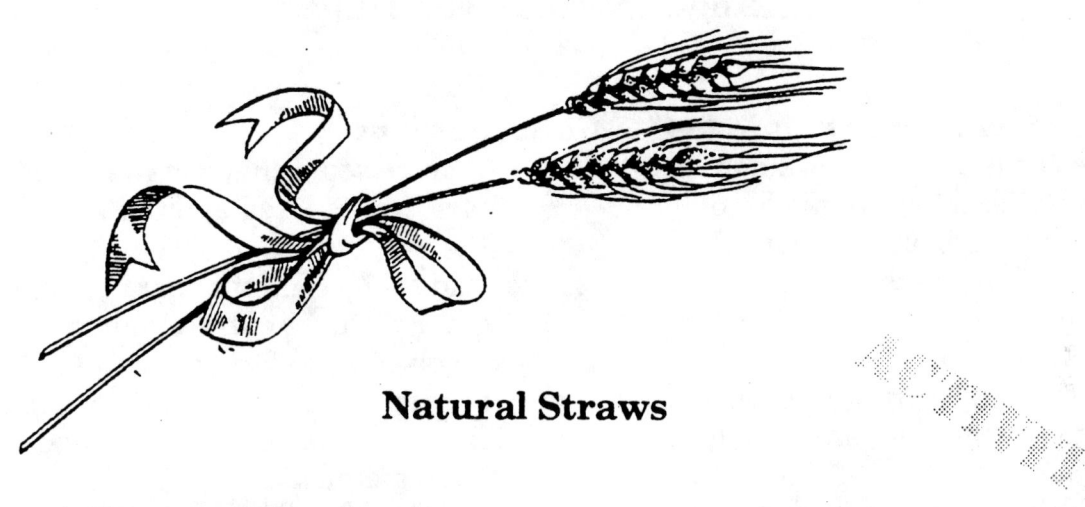

Natural Straws

Background information: Natural straws come from stalks of oats or wheat. They are hollow and can actually be used for drinking.

Procedures:
1. Find a farm with a field of oats or wheat.
2. Ask the farmer for permission to visit the farm. Talk to him or her about what you'd like to do. Also, ask about having the farmer spend some time with the children, talking about life on the farm and answering the children's questions.
3. Visit the farm when the oats or wheat is almost ready to be harvested. Take the children to the field and help them each carefully pick one stalk of grain (with the farmer's permission, of course).
4. Trim the tops and bottoms of the stalks. Cut the stalks to the size of a drinking straw.
5. Wash the stalks in clean water.
6. Use the straws for drinking.

Suggestions:
- Pack a picnic and have lunch outside when you visit the farm.
- If any of the children live on a farm, have them share some of the things they do on the farm and some of the things they like about living on a farm.
- Display pictures of farms, especially of crops in the field.
- Talk about what happens to the wheat and oats after it's harvested.

Follow-up:
- Send a thank you note to the farmer. Send along a picture of the children drinking from their straws.

Changes Throughout the Year

There are a number of different ways in which you might record seasonal changes throughout the year. Following are two suggestions.

Taking Pictures Over Time

Background information: A tree outside of the classroom window can serve as an excellent reminder of changes throughout the year. Use a camera to capture these changes.

Procedures:
1. Take a picture of the tree in the fall of the year, after the leaves have changed their color.
2. Take another picture in the winter, after the leaves have fallen and the limbs are covered with snow.
3. Take a picture in spring soon after the first small green leaves of the season appear.
4. Take a picture in summer showing the tree with full-grown leaves.
5. Display these pictures on a bulletin board.

Suggestions:
- Include some children in each of the pictures, dressed appropriately for the weather.
- Add to the bulletin board display, other pictures of the children involved in different seasonal activities—raking leaves, playing in the snow, planting flowers, and having a picnic.
- Enlarge these pictures and display them near the classroom window.
- Have the pictures made into slides and use them as an attention-getting way of focusing discussion on what the children see in the different pictures.

Follow-up:
- Use the slides for an end-of-the-year program, featuring a presentation of the various activities.

Dressing a Tree

Background information: A large four-panel display might be used to illustrate the changes taking place in a tree over the four seasons of the year. This display could be affixed to a bulletin board or wall space in the room, as an on-going feature of the room decor. An alternative is to prepare a four-section folding display which can be introduced at different times during the year. The display should be large enough to accommodate the children's art work.

Procedures:
1. Draw an outline of a tree (trunk and branches) on each of the four different panels.
2. During the fall of the year, have the children do leaf rubbings. Cut them out and attach them to the limbs of the tree. Also make a pile of paper or pressed leaves around or near the base of the tree.
3. During the winter, have children attach strips of cotton (snow) to the bare branches and along the trunk of the tree. They might also make snowmen figures (out of cotton or paper) to place around the tree.
4. During the spring, make small green leaves out of tissue paper. Have the children tear or cut the paper into small leaf-shaped pieces. Glue these to the branches of the tree. Add rain drops on and around the tree.
5. During the summer, attach larger leaves to the tree. Add paper flowers around the base of the tree and a sun behind the tree.

Suggestions:
- Keep all four panels on display throughout the year. Use the decorating of the tree as an indicator of the beginning of each new season.

Follow-up:
- Encourage children to make their own individual trees for each season, as well. Their individual trees could match the newly-decorated tree on the display board.

Suggested Children's Books

Keats, Ezra Jack. *THE SNOWY DAY.* Illustrations by author. Viking, 1962. 33 pages. Fiction Interest Level: Ages 3-7.

Hines, Anna Grossnickle. *COME TO THE MEADOW.* Illustrations by author. Clarion, 1984. Fiction. Interest Level: Ages 3-6.

Lionni, Leo. *FREDERICK.* Illustrations by author. Pantheon, 1967. Fiction. Interest Level: Ages 3-7.

Otto, Carolyn, *THAT SKY, THAT RAIN.* Illustrations by Megan Lloyd. Harper, 1990. Fiction. Interest Level: Ages 3-6.

Rockwell, Anne. *APPLES AND PUMPKINS.* Illustrations by Lizzy Rockwell. Macmillan, 1989. Fiction. Interest Level: Ages 2-6.

Welber, Robert. *THE WINTER PICNIC.* Illustrations by Deborah Ray. Pantheon, 1970. Fiction. Interest Level: Ages 3-6.

Allen, Marjorie N., and Shelley Rotner. *CHANGES.* Photos by Shelley Rotner. Macmillan, 1991. Nonfiction. Interest Level: Ages 3-5.

Selsam, Millicent, and Joyce Hunt. *KEEP LOOKING!* Illustrations by Normand Chartier, Macmillan, 1989. 32 pages. Nonfiction. Interest Level: Ages 3-7.

Aragon, Jane Chelsea. *WINTER HARVEST.* Illustrations by Leslie Baker. Little, 1988. Fiction. Interest Level: Ages 3-7.

Brinckloe, Julie. *FIREFLIES !* Illustrations by author. Macmillan, 1985. Fiction. Interest Level: Ages 5-9.

Recommended Resources

The Kid's Nature Book. S. Milford. Charlotte, VT: Williamson Publishing, 1989.

Marmalade Days (Fall, Winter, and Spring editions). C. Taylor-Bond. Livonia, MI: Partner Press, 1987

Earth Child. K. Sheehan, & m. Waidner. Tulsa, OK: Council Oak Books, 1991.Chapter 2.Earth Celebrations Throughout the Year

Outside Play and Learning Book, The. K. Miller. Mt. Rainier, MD: Gryphon House, 1989.

Grow Lab: A Complete Guide to Gardening in the Classroom. E. Pranis, J. Hale.: Burlington, VT: National Gardening Association, 1991.

Learning About Food

Implementation Guideline # 7: Demonstrate the connection between the food we eat and the world of nature.

Understanding that many of our foods come from plants can help children grow in appreciation of the natural world. A number of different activities can help children make the connection between the foods we eat and the world of nature. Such activities could include visiting farms, gardens, and orchards; planting a garden or even just a few vegetable plants; watching a homemaker can fruits or vegetables; and assisting in the food preparation process, especially in preparing foods from raw fruits and vegetables.

Food items should be always treated with respect. They are gifts from nature and essential for our life. Food should never be wasted nor used for play. It should be handled carefully and served in a respectful way. From the way we present and handle food, children can learn that our need for and use of food are concrete examples of how we are linked to the rest of the natural world.

Following are some suggestions on how to help children understand the connection between the food we eat and the world of nature.

Growing "Food Plants"

Background information: Given the right conditions, some foods will sprout and grow into lovely plants. These plants become a source of fascination and observation for the children, and make delightful room decorations, as well. Several "food plants" that might be grown in the classroom are the sweet potato vine, a variety of citrus foods, pineapple, and carrot.

Procedures for a sweet potato vine:
1. To grow a sweet potato vine, look for a sweet potato that is old, firm, and plump. If you can find one that has sprouts already growing, choose that one.
2. Place the sweet potato in a clear glass jar, which will allow the children to see the roots as they develop. Place the thinner part of the potato (i.e., the tapered end) in the jar, with about one-half of the potato extending over the top.
3. Stick four toothpicks into the sides of the potato to hold the potato in place.
4. Put just enough water in the jar to cover the end of the potato.
5. Keep the potato in a dark place for about ten days. Check to see that the water level remains constant during this time.
6. After the ten-day dark period, place the potato in a warm, sunny spot.
7. Wait until the shoots are several inches long, then clip all but about four of the sturdiest shoots. Clipping the plant back in this way, allows for healthier growth.
8. If the season permits, plant the potato outdoors once it begins to cave in. Expect the sweet potato to last for several months before all its food supply is used up and it begins to cave.

Procedures for citrus plants:
1. Save the seeds from grapefruits, oranges, tangerines, or lemons.
2. Soak the seeds in warm water for 8 to 10 hours.
3. Plant the seeds in a shallow container (e.g., egg carton or meat tray).
4. Cover the seeds with about 1/4 inch of soil, and water enough to make the soil moist.
5. Keep the planter in a warm, dark place. Check everyday to see that the soil is kept moist.
6. Keep the seedlings in their original planter until they sprout two pairs of leaves. Once these leaves appear, separate the seedlings and plant in individual pots.
7. Give the plants a few days to adjust, then move them to a sunny warm window.
8. Enjoy the dark green, glossy leaves and the minimal care required to keep them healthy in the classroom.

Procedures for a pineapple plant:
1. Cut off the crown of a pineapple plant with about 1/2 inch of the pineapple fruit remaining.
2. Pull off any dead leaves and allow the top to dry for one to two weeks.
3. Plant the crown about one inch deep in a pot of sand.
4. Keep the sand moist.
5. Once roots have developed, plant the pineapple in a pot of soil. First, prepare the planter for drainage by placing small rocks in the bottom of the pot. Then fill with good potting soil and use some type of plant fertilizer.
6. Provide a place for the pineapple where it can get good light and moist air.
7. Water the leaves and crown with a mist spray bottle. Also, keep the soil around the plant somewhat moist.

Procedures for a carrot plant.
1. Choose a fresh carrot with the leafy top still attached. Avoid carrots with root hairs showing.
2. Cut back the top within one inch of the carrot.
3. Cut most of the carrot away, leaving only about 1/2 inch.
4. Place this piece in a shallow dish, with some pebbles or stones around it to hold it in place.
5. Add water to the dish to where it is level with the top of the carrot. Keep the water level constant.
6. Invert a plastic tumbler over the top to help keep the plant moist.
7. Place the dish near a sunny window and watch the carrot top grow.

Suggestions:
- Read *The Carrot Seed* by Ruth Krauss in connection with the carrot activity.
- Use a magnifying glass to look more closely at the roots, seeds, and leaves of the plants.

Follow-up:
- Add a variety of seeds and rinds to the "Discovery Center". Observe the rinds over a period of several days to note changes.
- With the children's help, write a "Big Book" about the food plant experience.

Enjoying Raw Vegetables

Background information: While vegetables aren't often the food of choice for young children, there are many things that can be done to make vegetables a more interesting and desirable food for them. Probably the best way to get children interested in eating and enjoying vegetables is to get them involved in the growing, harvesting, and preparation process.

Procedures:
1. Visit a road-side stand or vegetable market.
2. Involve the children in selecting vegetables to take back to school.
3. Once back in the classroom, work with the children in cleaning the vegetables and preparing them for snack or lunch.
4. Prepare a vegetable dip and invite the children to taste a variety of the vegetables.

Suggestions:
- Call attention to the variety of colors, textures, and tastes.
- Display pictures of vegetable gardens.

Follow-up:
- Introduce new vegetables over a period of time. When possible, introduce as much of the plant as possible, versus just a piece of the vegetable (e.g. a head of cauliflower versus bit-size pieces of cauliflower).
- Involve the children in making homemade vegetable soup.

Finding Seeds in Food

Background information: Most plants produce seeds which may grow into new plants of the same type. A variety of fruits and vegetables can be studied as a way of finding out more information about seeds and the vital link between the natural world and our food supply.

Procedures:
1. Introduce a variety of fruits and vegetables for children to study, eat, and enjoy. Encourage a close observation of the seeds inside.
2. Have children compare the seeds (e.g., the size, shape, color, hardness, etc.) from different foods.

Suggestions:
- Use a magnifying glass to look more closely at the seeds and the part of the plant that holds the seeds.
- Introduce a variety of seeds that we eat—corn, peas, sunflower seeds, etc. When possible, introduce the plants or parts of the plants from which these seeds come.
- Before cutting open a banana, ask the children if there are seeds inside. Provide plastic knives and then let them explore and discover on their own.

Follow-up:
- Save melon and pumpkin seeds. Let the children wash and dry them.

Finding the New Plant in an Onion Bulb

Background information: A bulb is an underground bud from which certain plants grow. In season, a bulb can be sliced open to reveal the plant inside.

Procedures:
1. Find a sprouting onion.
2. Slice it open vertically.
3. Encourage the children to observe the new plant inside the bulb.

Suggestions:
- If possible, give each child a sprouting onion. Help them slice it open. Let them discover the new plant inside their own onion. Show interest in the children's comments about the smell, the feel, and the juiciness of the onion.

Follow-up:
- Allow the onions to set out overnight. Encourage the children to note changes in the onions from the day before.
- Use an onion half to make onion prints with tempera paint.

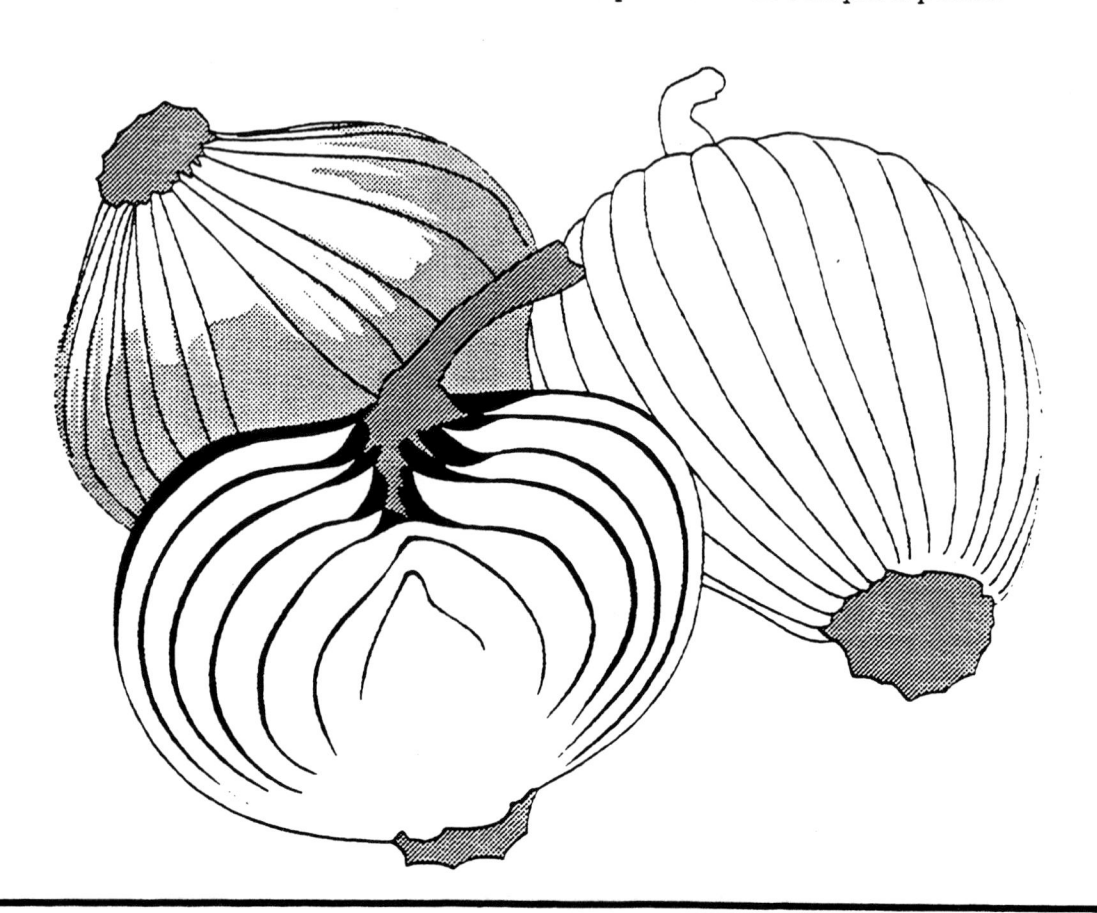

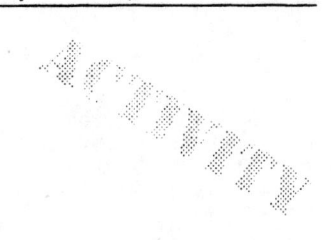

Discovering How Plants Drink

Background information: Young children may know that plants need water to live. What they may not know is how plants drink. "Where's their mouth?" is a logical question for a three-year-old to ask. A piece of celery and some colored water might help them discover how plants take in water.

Procedures:
1. Place a stalk of celery in a jar of colored water. Choose a stalk with leaves attached.
2. Wait for about an hour, then check the tips of the leaves for signs of color.
3. Once color is observed, slice the stalk of celery lengthwise.
4. Help the children find the color through the entire length of the stalk.

Suggestions:
- Allow plenty of time for observation and discussion. Avoid telling the children that the water moved up the stem; let them discover it on their own.
- Provide a magnifying glass for closer observation.

Follow-up:
- Share information about this activity with the parents. Encourage them to do a "repeat performance" at home.
- Once the children discovered what happened in the stalk of celery, use an eye dropper or baster to illustrate a similar action.

Making Flour

Background information: Flour, to many children, is something you buy in a bag at the grocery store. Few may realize that flour comes from grains, or seeds.

Procedures:
1. Secure several cups of wheat.
2. Give each child a paper plate (or sheet of paper), several grains of wheat, and a small stone.
3. Have the children place the wheat on the paper and then pound it gently with the stone.
4. Once the wheat is ground, have the children feel it, smell it, and taste it.

Suggestions:
- Before grinding the wheat, let the children chew several of the grains. Encourage them to talk about the taste and the texture.
- For a larger quantity of flour, use a food blender with the capacity for grinding wheat. Refer to blender instructions for specific directions.
- Display whole stalks of wheat. Examine the roots, stems, leaves, and head.
- Decorate the classroom with stalks of wheat.
- Examine a slice of whole wheat bread with a magnifying glass.
- Look for pictures of wheat on bread bags and cereal boxes. Share these with the children.

Follow-up:
- Use some of the flour to make cookies.
- Plant some of the kernels in pots of soil.

Homemade Peanut Butter

Background information: Most children are familiar with peanut butter, but many may not know that peanut butter is made from peanuts. Homemade peanut butter can be made by simply grinding peanuts.

Procedures:
1. Obtain a bag of peanuts in the shell.
2. Involve the children in shelling the peanuts.
3. Allow time for tasting and smelling.
4. Grind the peanuts in a blender according to blender directions.

Suggestions:
- Display pictures of a peanut plant.
- Display as a group: jars of peanuts in the shell, shelled peanuts, and peanut butter.

Follow-up:
- Toast some bread and enjoy the world's freshest peanut butter!

Toasting Pumpkin Seeds

Background information: Few people would be interested in eating raw pumpkin seeds, but once toasted, pumpkin seeds are quite good.

Procedures:
1. When carving a pumpkin, save the seeds.
2. Wash the seeds and lay them out to dry for a day or two.
3. Spread the seeds, single layer, on a cookie sheet.
4. Bake in an oven set at low temperature for 20-30 minutes.
5. Sprinkle with a little salt and enjoy a nutritious snack.

Suggestions:
- If an oven is not available, toast the pumpkin seeds in a skillet. First melt a few teaspoons of margarine over low heat and then stir the seeds until lightly browned.
- Make toasting pumpkin seeds a part of a larger unit on learning about pumpkins. Start with a visit to a pumpkin patch and end with the eating of pumpkin pie.

Follow-up:
- Add toasted pumpkin seeds to a cookie dough mix and bake some pumpkin seed cookies.

Enjoying Rice

Background information: Rice is one of the world's most important food crops, with about half the people of the world eating this grain as their chief food. Many people in Asia eat rice three times a day, and often have little else to eat. In some of the oriental countries, rice cakes are eaten at certain festivals as symbols of happiness and long life. The rice plant is a type of grass, unfamiliar to many children. While some rice is grown in the United States (especially in Arkansas, California, Texas, and Louisiana), most of the world's rice supply is grown in Asia. Children can learn more about rice in a variety of hands-on activities. Some ways to enjoy rice include pouring and stirring rice in the texture table, floating rice in the water table, and putting rice inside jars for making "noise-makers" or maracas. Rice can also be enjoyed by cooking and eating. For a special treat, try rice pudding or glorified rice.

Procedures:
1. Gather the following ingredients.
   1 8 3/4-ounce can crushed pineapple
   2/3 cup precooked rice
   2 teaspoons lemon juice
   1 1/2 cups miniature marshmallows
   1 ripe banana, sliced
   1 cup whipping cream, whipped
   2 tablespoons chopped maraschino cherries
2. Drain the pineapple, reserving the syrup.
3. In saucepan, combine the uncooked rice, 2/3 cup water, pineapple syrup, and 1/2 teaspoon salt.
4. Stir to moisten the rice.
5. Bring rice and liquid quickly to a boil.
6. Cover and simmer five minutes.
7. Add pineapple and lemon juice.
8. Cool this mixture.
9. Stir in marshmallows and bananas.
10. Fold in cream and cherries.
11. Chill a second time.
12. Enjoy a delicious desert.

Suggestions:
- Complete in advance Steps 1 through 8. Complete Steps 9 through 12 with the children.
- Find and display pictures of rice fields.

Follow-up:
- Collect other recipes for rice and then; introduce a variety of rice dishes to the children. Ask parents to share their favorite rice dish recipe.

Popping Popcorn

Background information: Popcorn is a fascinating food. The unpopped kernels are hard and shiny—not at all edible for humans. When popped, however, it becomes a delightful snack. Popcorn kernels contain over 10% moisture. When heated, the moisture changes into steam. The hard covering on the kernel keeps the steam from escaping. Pressure builds up to where the kernel pops.

Procedures:
1. Introduce popcorn on the cob to children.
2. Solicit the children's help in shelling the corn. While doing so, discuss the color, texture, and size of the popcorn kernels. Compare the popcorn seed to other seeds.
3. Pop the corn in a popcorn popper.
4. Enjoy a delicious snack.

Suggestions:
- Visit a farm or garden where popcorn is grown. Let children explore the popcorn plant.
- Read *The Popcorn Book* by Tomie dePaola.
- Compare the size of bag needed to hold popcorn once it's popped to the size of bag needed in its unpopped stage.

Follow-up:
- Serve unpopped kernels and leftover popcorn to the birds.

Cracking a Coconut

Background information: The coconut is one of the largest seeds that grows. It grows inside a hard brown shell. The seed itself is a ball of crisp, white, sweet-tasting "meat" covered by a tough brown skin. The coconut has a hollow center, which holds a sugary liquid called coconut milk. Both the milk and the meat are edible.

Procedures:
1. Before cracking a coconut, take time to explore its size, weight, color, and texture.
2. Show pictures of coconuts growing on trees.
3. When ready to crack the coconut, puncture the soft spots at the end of it and drain the milk.
4. The next step is to crack the shell. This step is not easy and usually requires some type of heavy tool, such as a hammer.
5. Once the coconut is cracked, scrape out pieces of the meat for all the children to taste. The coconut milk can be tasted, too, although most of the children will probably not want more than just a taste.

Suggestions:
- Display the coconut for a few days before cracking it open. Display it along with other foods that grow on trees (apples, citrus fruits, pears, etc.).
- Keep the coconut shell on display for a few days after cracking it open. Encourage the children to explore it along with shells and rinds from other foods (peanut shells, orange peels, etc.)

Follow-up:
- Chop some of the coconut meat into small pieces and mix with cookie dough. Bake and enjoy the cookies.
- Sprinkle the chopped coconut over icing on cookies or cupcakes.

Suggested Children's Books

McMillan, Bruce. *GROWING COLORS*. Photos by author. Lothrop, 1988. Nonfiction. Interest Level: Ages 2-6.

Wexler, Jerome. *FLOWERS, FRUITS, SEEDS*. Photos by author. Prentice, 1987. Nonfiction. Interest Level: Ages 2-6.

Caseley, Judith. *GRANDPA'S GARDEN LUNCH*. Illustrations by author. Greenwillow, 1990. Fiction. Interest Level: Ages 3-6.

Titherington, Jeanne. *PUMPKIN PUMPKIN*. Illustrations by author. Greenwillow, 1986. 24 pages. Fiction. Interest Level: Ages 2-6.

Recommended Resources

Plantworks. K. Shanberg, & S. Tekiela. Cambridge, MN: Adventure Publications, 1991.

Earth Child. K. Sheehan, & M. Waidner. Tulsa OK: Council Oak Books, 1991. Chapter 3. Wonders in a Garden

Your First Garden Book. M. Brown.: Little, 1981

In My Garden: A Child's Gardening Book. H. Oechsli, & K. Oechsli. : Macmillan, 1985.

Group Activities

Implementation Guideline # 8: Introduce a variety of nature-related themes and concepts through group activities.

While group activities tend to be more teacher-directed than free play or center time, the experience for the child should still be one of hands-on, active involvement. It's important for teachers to remember that children learn by doing, not by listening and watching. Group activities, then, must allow for a great deal of active participation on the part of the children. To be avoided are lists of "dos and don'ts" which will interfere with the child's engagement in the activity. Also to be avoided are large group sizes or the type of activities that require children to do a lot of waiting for their turn to participate. Groups of five or six tend to be more successful than groups of eleven or twelve, and children are generally more satisfied if they aren't required to wait for more than five minutes before it's their turn to do an activity.

Teachers need to plan group activities that engage children both cognitively and affectively. The activities must provide opportunities for learning in multimodal ways (i.e., through intellectual discovery, sensorial experiences, and emotional engagement; through art, movement, stories, dramatic play, etc.). Such an approach to teaching and learning is sometimes referred to as being holistic in nature and matches well the guidelines for developmentally appropriate practices as outlined by the National Association for the Education of Young Children (Bredekamp, 1987). The teacher, in leading group activities, must be more of a facilitator and a consultant than an instructor. Children must be given the opportunity to experiment and discover on their own. Telling the children about nature versus setting the stage for them to discover and experience the wonders of nature is not an appropriate approach to environmental education with preschool children.

Group activities need to be warm, comfortable, and fun. They need to focus on what is of interest to children.

One concern that most teachers face is what to do with the child who chooses not to participate in a group activity. Should children be given the choice of non-participation? An understanding of child development and the uniqueness of each individual suggest that requiring the whole class to participate in all the planned group activities would not be appropriate. What is important and appropriate for fostering the growth and development of young children is recognition of their interests and efforts. Jenny may choose not to do a bark rubbing, but may enjoy raking the leaves in the school yard. Both are nature-related activities and both can lead to a greater appreciation of the natural world. Jenny needs to be recognized for what she is ready to do, and not made to feel incompetent or "bad" for what she is not interested in at the present time. Jenny's involvement with nature (i.e., raking leaves) can be recognized through something as simple as a positive comment. "Jenny's made a big pile of leaves. Let's ask her if we can jump in it."

The Sharing Circle: Learning to Show Respect

Background information: The "Sharing Circle" is a form of Show-and-Tell and is a popular group activity in many early childhood programs. Through this activity, the children and the teacher(s) take turns sharing with the group what is of interest and/or of importance to them. To be effective and meaningful, this activity requires a respectful listening to the one showing and talking about what they have to share. While sitting still and listening is usually perceived as a passive activity—and often difficult for young children to do—respecting what is of value to another person requires active participation on the part of the other children in the group. Even young children can learn that showing respect means more than just waiting for their turn to speak. Showing respect means to honor and show esteem. It involves recognizing and appreciating the feelings of others for what is important and of value to them. One way to foster the development of respect is through an "About Me" activity.

Procedures:

1. Ask each child to bring in a picture of themselves when they were a baby. Have them also find out something special about themselves when they were a baby (e.g. liked to eat graham crackers dipped in milk; always carried a teddy bear around the house; liked to play with Daddy's shoes, etc.). Parents will need to help with this activity and can be informed of the request and the reason for it by way of a newsletter or flyer.
2. As the baby pictures come in, mount each one in a special frame.
3. On the day of the Sharing Circle (and after all the pictures are in), start by showing the children a picture of a baby in a magazine or book. Tell the children that, while the baby in the picture may be very cute, the picture itself is not really special to you, because you don't know that baby.
4. Show them a picture of yourself as a baby. Tell them that this picture is very important to you—and even more important to your mother! This picture's important because it's you—not someone else you don't even know. Also, tell them something about yourself as a baby.
5. After you're finished sharing, praise the children for showing an interest in you and in what is special and important to you. Explain to the children that they were showing respect when they listened quietly. Let them know that you felt honored and happy when they showed respect.
6. Invite each child to show his or her baby picture and to tell something about themselves when they were babies.

7. Ask the other children to listen quietly and show respect. Remind them that such respect honors the person speaking.

Suggestions:
- Keep the group for Sharing Circles small. Many children will not be able to sit still throughout the entire activity if more than 5 or 6 children need to take turns for sharing.
- Lead Sharing Circles focusing on a variety of nature-related items brought in by the children. Invite them to bring in something they like or found interesting—maybe it's something from their yard, a favorite book about animals, or pictures of something they like in nature (e.g., flowers, trees, lakes, etc.). Emphasize respect for nature and for each other throughout the activity.
- Use the Sharing Circle format to introduce interesting things that you have from nature—e.g., a cicada shell, a pea pod, an abandoned bird's nest, a beautiful flower, etc.

Follow-up:
- If show-and-tell time is used, not only for learning interesting things about the natural world, but also for fostering behaviors demonstrating honor and respect, this component of the early childhood experience may prove to be one of the most beneficial parts of the program. Once people learn to respect and honor the world around them, chances of living in peace and harmony with the natural environment and with other people will be greatly enhanced. Emphasize honor and respect throughout every part of the day.

Animal Tracks

Background information: Once children become aware of how the presence of animals can often be detected by the tracks they leave behind, they may enjoy some simple games focusing on animal tracks as a theme. One such game can be played using playdough and castings of animal tracks.

Procedures:
1. Roll out playdough to cover a surface about the size of an open book or larger.
2. Use castings of animal tracks or rubber stamps of animal tracks to make markings in the playdough.
3. Tell a story about the animals as you make tracks on the playdough (e.g., These tracks show that a deer and a rabbit walked along the same path. They went to the pond to get a drink.)
4. While the rest of the group turns away from the table so that they can't see what is being done, one child makes a few simple animal tracks in the playdough.
5. Another child is chosen to match the castings or stamps to the tracks and to suggest what "story" was left behind.
6. Children continue taking turns as long as interest dictates.

Suggestions:
- Incorporate discussion about the size of the footprints, the length of the path, and possible reasons why an animal would choose one path over another (e.g., to remain hidden, to find food, to find material for building a nest, etc.).
- Display books about animals, especially books about animal behavior.

Follow-up:
- Look for animal tracks outdoors. Follow them as far as you can. Talk about the story behind the tracks.

The Hiding Game

Background information: The theme of the Hiding Game is camouflage. While young children may not be familiar with this term, they may have noticed (perhaps with your help!) that some animals, because of their coloring, are hard to find. They may not readily notice the bird perched on the branch of the tree because its feathers are almost the same color as the bark. The walking stick and praying mantis are other good examples of how the animal's coloring makes it difficult to find the animal. If children have not had a chance to study the effect of camouflage in the natural environment, you can set up the opportunity in the classroom.

Procedures:
1. Find a simple-to-get animal for this activity—a small turtle or crayfish would work well.
2. Display the animal in a natural-like setting that matches its color. This might be done inside an aquarium. You might use twigs, leaves, grasses, etc. to build the habitat.
3. Then place the animal in a setting with contrasting colors.
4. Talk about the differences in how well you see the animal in the two different settings. Also talk about the advantage of the camouflage.

Suggestions:
- Take pictures of the animal in the two different settings. Study the pictures and discuss the differences you see.
- If you do not have a live animal to demonstrate the effect of camouflage, you may be able to find some good pictures to share with the children. You could laminate the pictures and place them in contrasting settings. You could also use realistic animal figurines, a piece of fake fur to represent a rabbit or other animals with fur, or different colored feathers to represent birds.

Follow-up:
- Use representations of one or more different small animals (rabbit, mouse, bird, etc.) and a variety of habitat areas (wooded, grassland, meadow, etc.). Have the children take turns hiding an "animal" of their choice. The goal is to place the animal in a habitat where its coloring makes it difficult to detect. For the sake of the game, the animal may not be hidden completely out of site (e.g., under a log). Everyone else closes their eyes while the animal is being hidden. They then try to find the animal.

Additional Group Activities

For additional group activities, you may wish to consider holding celebration parties to honor special occasions. Such occasions could include the first day of a new season, Earth Day (April 22), or Sun Day (May 3, a good day to plant a sunflower). You might also role play certain phenomena in nature, such as the life cycle of a frog or a butterfly. For the butterfly, you could let children take turns wrapping up in a sheet to represent the pupal stage and then emerging with colorful scarves in their hands to represent the coming out of a butterfly.

Recommended Resources

Sharing the Joy of Nature. J. Cornell. Nevada City, CA: Dawn Publications, 1989.

Sharing the Joy of Nature (video) J. Cornell. Nevada City, CA: Dawn Publications, 1991.

Sharing Nature with Children. J. Cornell. Nevada City, CA: Dawn Publications, 1979.

Outside Play and Learning Book, The. K. Miller. Mt. Rainier, MD: Gryphon House, 1989.

Part II: Implementing the Curriculum

Enriching the Classroom Environment

Implementation Guideline # 9: Display nature-related art and use materials from the natural world to decorate the classroom.

There are many things that can be done to bring the world of nature indoors. In the early childhood classroom, plants, animals, and nature-related room decorations might be used. Special displays could highlight the different seasons of the year. The best kinds of displays are ones that offer something for the children to do (not just see!) and are related to what the children have done (e.g., visited a greenhouse and helped in deciding which plants to get for the terrarium).

A Terrarium for the Classroom

Background information: A terrarium is especially nice to have in the classroom, as it requires little care and accommodates a variety of plants, including moss—a plant that may be new to some of the children.

Procedures:
1. Start by placing a large glass container where you plan to display it, as it may be too heavy to move easily once it is filled. A sunny location is not necessary.
2. Spread some colorful sand or tiny stones on the bottom to add color and interest. You may wish to build up one side more than the other—again to add interest.
3. Add a layer of potting soil, about two inches deep.
4. Plant several small house plants of varying sizes in the terrarium.
5. Add small shells, rocks, or pieces of driftwood for decoration.
6. Sprinkle water on the plants and soil.
7. Cover the tank securely with clear plastic. Poke two to three small holes in the plastic.

Suggestions:
- While any large glass container can be used for a terrarium, a fish tank is especially good, as it is watertight.
- In addition to the terrarium, display other ways for indoor plants to grow—e.g., clippings in a glass or water, seedlings in a plastic cup, vines from a sweet potato, etc.

Follow-up:
- Set up a cactus display in an open glass container. Use sand and small colored stones as a base.

Room Decorations

Nature-related room decorations could include photos and posters depicting scenes from nature, as well as real items from nature including drift wood, pine cones, dried grasses, shells, and pebbles. Nature-related room decorations should also include children's artwork. In fact, an early childhood classroom should have children's art displayed at all times, and these displays should change frequently.

Children's nature-related art should be expressions of their own feelings and understandings about the beauty and mystery of nature. Much of this art should be in the form of spontaneous drawings and paintings. While the emphasis should always be on the process (the doing) versus the product (what it represents), children may wish, at times, to label their art—that is they may freely tell you what their art represents. When children do so, it's good to label their work of art as such.

The Earth Flag

Beautiful Earth flags are now available in a variety of sizes and usually feature a photo-like image of Earth floating in space in its natural state, without borders or political boundaries. To help children appreciate the wonder and beauty of Earth, it is recommended that an Earth flag be displayed in a prominent place in every classroom. Earth flags are available from several different sources, including the SaveEnergy Company, 2410 Harrison Street, San Francisco, CA 94110. A toll-free number to call is 800-326-2120.

Also available through the Save Energy Company are an Earth Ball, a Wildlife Ball, and Hugg-a-Planet. The Hugg-a-Planet is a soft, colorful stuffed Earth, featuring color-coded vegetation. The Earth Ball and Wildlife Ball are plastic balls, the one featuring Planet Earth without borders or boundaries, the other native animals in their natural habitats. Similar nature-related toys are available through other educational and environmental companies and can add beauty and interest to an early childhood classroom.

Friends of Flagship Earth also make Earth Flags available to qualifying schools. Their flag, the Children's Global Flag, features a blue planet surrounded by a golden-yellow aura. The blue on the flag stands for proper stewardship of Planet Earth; the golden-yellow for the natural beauty of all cultures and colors of children living on Earth. For information on how your school can be awarded the Children's Global Flag, write to: Friends of Flagship Earth, c/o The Flagship Earth Foundation, 65 Washington Street, #200, Santa Clara, CA 95050.

Designing a Classroom

Should you ever be in a position to design a classroom when building or remodeling, keep closeness to nature in mind. Following are some physical features that could help children see and feel closer to nature:
- low windows
- window seats
- freedom to move directly outdoors from the classroom.

"The clearest way into the universe is through a forest wilderness."
John Muir

Chapter 5

Outdoor Excursions

Field Trips

Implementation Guideline # 10: Go on a variety of nature-study field trips.

Guidelines for Fun and Safety

The following basic guidelines are designed to enhance the child's safety and enjoyment when participating in outdoor activities, while at the same time, fostering appreciation and respect for the natural world.

1. See that the children are dressed appropriately. The children's clothing should help protect them against cold, sun, and skin irritations (due to scratches, bites, poison ivy, etc.). Care should be taken, however, to avoid over-dressing the children. Over-dressing will get in the way of experiencing the world of nature through touch.

2. Keep all the children within sight at all times. While this may be easy to do when playing in the school yard, it becomes a little more challenging when exploring a wooded or hilly area. When venturing beyond the school yard, extra adults should always be considered. Each adult should then know exactly which children he or she is responsible for. While the children should not be expected to do everything in a group, the whereabouts of each child should be known at all times.

3. Check out the conditions of an anticipated excursion site before leading a group of children to the site. Know whether or not bathrooms are available, where the nearest phone is located, and how easy or difficult it is to move around in the area (Are there well-defined trails? Do the trails tend to be muddy? Are there guard rails or other safeguards, where needed—e.g., life guards for swimming or wading areas; safe, easy-to-manage stairs, etc.?).

4. Build in ample opportunities for hands-on involvement. Avoid situations where children are expected to listen for extended periods of time and are not given

opportunities for active participation.
5. Whenever entering a natural area, remind the children that this is where many living creatures live and that we must respect their homes. We must be careful not to destroy or disturb the natural area unnecessarily. Respecting the home of natural animals and plants means not removing or rearranging things in the natural environment. If we turn over a log or rock to study the animals living underneath, it's important to return the log or rock to its original position. If we want to use some seeds or dried grasses in a collage, we'll take only what we need and not disturb the rest.
6. Set a few (but only a few!) field trip rules. The following are offered as suggestions:
    - Don't hurt anyone or anything.
    - Always stay close to the group.
    - Don't pick or take anything without permission.
7. Encourage quiet observation. "Still-hunting" is an exercise suggested by Joseph Cornell (1979) in *Sharing Nature With Children* as a way of helping children enter into a state of quiet observation. In "still-hunting", you become as motionless as you can, so that the natural world around you goes on as if you weren't there. During periods of quiet observation, you are more likely to see a number of wild animals that would otherwise remain hidden from view.

One early childhood educator uses the idea of "quiet retreat" when introducing the children to the practice of quiet observation. She tells the children that natural areas are special places and that this "specialness" can be experienced and appreciated only when you quiet yourself—both inside and outside. She encourages rollicking play in open spaces but suggests quiet observation, or a quiet retreat, in the woods and meadows. Thus, she attunes the children to a spirit of quiet observation and encourages behaviors which are non-threatening to the animals.

What to Look For

Excursions in the out-of-doors have a high probability of being successful, even if you have not planned in advance what you want the children to see or experience. If children are encouraged to be active explorers and if their discoveries are attended to, they will find enough on their own to make the trip a valuable learning experience. If taught to become good observers of the world around them, young children will find the bird nests, ant hills, frozen puddles, tracks in the snow, tree branches dancing in the wind, and squirrels running circles around the tree trunks.

Once a child has called attention to what he or she has observed, you might enhance the learning experience by adding comments about what you observe or asking the child some "what do you think" questions (e.g., "Why do you think the sidewalk feels warmer than the grass?). You can also encourage the children to find descriptive words for what they observe and experience. Is the bark rough or smooth? How does the sand feel? Did you hear the splash when the frog jumped in the pond?

To help children become good observers of the environment, you can encourage them to look for changes— changes from one season to another, changes from one day to the next, changes from the morning to the afternoon, changes in plants, changes in the weather, etc. If they notice a crack in the dry earth one day, you might encourage them to look at the same crack several days in a row to see if it gets bigger or smaller or goes away.

You can also encourage children to look for ways in which things in the natural world are connected, or relate to each other. You might help them discover that plants grow toward the sun, rain washes the sand out of the sandbox, birds use dry grass to build their nests, etc. The fact that everything in nature is connected is one of the most important ecological concepts that we can impart to young children, for it is this understanding that leads one to the conclusion that everything is part of a whole and all things—no matter how small—are worthy of respect.

In addition to looking for signs of how things change and how they're related to each other, you can also encourage children to look for what is beautiful and what makes them feel happy. When given the opportunity and encouragement to express their feelings about what they see as beautiful in nature, many young children will freely talk about such things as watching butterflies dance over flowers, listening to a bubbling brook, smelling wildflowers, and walking barefoot through the grass.

How to Keep Children Actively Involved

Young children learn by acting on their environment. They need to feel, manipulate, and hold in their hands. When outdoors, they'll want to pick, poke, and squash things. Keeping young children actively involved without allowing them to harm the natural environment is a challenge, indeed.

Following are some techniques that might be used to, not only keep young children actively involved, but also enhance their enjoyment of the natural world.

1. Give each child a small spray bottle filled with water. Tell the children that they might want to spray a little bit of water on such things as dried leaves, a handful of earth, wildflowers, etc. Ask them if they notice any differences after they've made it wet. Does it smell any different? Does it look any different? Does it feel any different? Spraying water gives children something to do and effects some noticeable changes in their environment. This type of hands-on involvement is healthy, in that it does not harm the environment and enhances the children's experience.

2. Focus attention on a well-defined area. Mark off a plot of land (about 6 feet by three feet) with a piece of string or yarn. Place tongue depressors (or some other type of stick) at the four corners of the area. Use these as posts to attach the string or yarn. Assign one or two children to each of the areas. Tell them that they have five minutes to discover as many different things as they can in their plot of land. After five minutes, call time for a "sharing circle" and have children talk about their discoveries.

3. Focus attention by using special "cameras" or "viewers" for looking at interesting things in the out-of-doors. Empty toilet tissue tubes make great "cameras." Looking through the tube isolates the

object being studied and blocks out surrounding views. The camera or viewer focuses attention and allows children to see an object or area much clearer and in more detail.

4. Focus attention by using sound-catchers. Sound-catchers are extensions of the outer ear and help collect and focus environmental sounds. Sound-catchers can be made by cutting the bottoms out of paper cups. These cups are then held against the ear, with the smaller opening (the bottom of the cup) over the ear. The larger opening (the top of the cup) helps to funnel sound waves into the ear.

5. Encourage children to find something small from the natural environment that they can hold in their hand while walking. They are to choose only non-living objects (e.g., a twig, dried leaf or seed, pine cone, pebble, etc). Children are encouraged to hold that object with respect and to get to know that object well before the end of the nature walk. Holding the object in their hand will keep that hand occupied and will remind the children to be attentive to the sights, feels, and smells of things in nature. After the nature walk has ended, ask the children to put all their objects in a pile. There will most likely be duplicates of certain objects. Because of the individual characteristics of each object, however, no two things will be exactly alike. The children then take turns identifying their own object and telling the rest of the group something special about what they carried during the nature walk (e.g., the stone is very smooth and has a red spot on one side of it).

Following are some additional ideas on how to keep children actively involved.

- smelling a variety of things—flowers, pine, dirt, etc.
- looking through, under, into, and around objects
- viewing things from different perspectives—from above, beside, under, etc.
- matching colors and shapes of things found in nature
- feeling the texture of many different things—moss, leaves, bark, sand, the back of a turtle, stones, etc.
- imitating the way things in nature move—run like the wind, hop like a bunny, sway like the tree branches, dance like the butterflies, etc.
- focusing attention on, or looking for, specific things (e.g., melting snow, bursting seed pods, new seedlings, animal tracks, animal homes, etc.)
- inviting children to show and talk about what they find interesting, versus listening to what you know

What to Take Along

While you'll want to avoid carrying a heavy or bulky pack when taking the children on outdoor excursions, there are some basic items that you may wish to have with you in a "discovery bag." The use of a back pack is suggested for the discovery bag, so that your hands remain free. Following is a list of suggested items to include in your discovery bag.

- collecting bottles (small plastic bottles with lids—some with "breathing holes")
- collecting bags (small paper bags—one for each child or pair of children)
- sifting screens
- camera
- magnifying glasses (one for each child or pair of children)

Follow-up Activities

In planning for an outdoor excursion, many teachers try to think of things they can do to prepare the children for the experience. They plan activities designed to introduce related vocabulary. They talk to the children about what they'll see on the trip. They sometimes read stories and provide picture books related to the outdoor excursion. While such plans are usually very well-intentioned, they're often in conflict with the way young children learn.

Young children learn by moving from concrete to representational experiences—that is, children need to first experience a real object before they can learn from a representation (photo, drawing, word, etc.) of that object. In learning about the natural world, children need to first experience a **real** object from nature before they will have an understanding of what that object is. In learning about things that live in water, for example, children should first visit a stream or pond and spend time observing the living creatures there. After they've had the experience of what is real, they can move on to activities that are representational (e.g., reading stories about minnows, painting pictures of fish, etc.)

Sharing Circle. Follow-up activities are probably more important than pre-trip activities. One follow-up activity which may help young children recall some of the experiences from their outdoor excursions involves a group sharing of "What I Remember" or "What I Liked." Children are asked to sit quietly in a circle and close their eyes for a few minutes. They are asked to think about their outdoor experience—what did they see; what did they hear; what did they feel; how did it make them feel, etc. After a minute or two, ask the children to open their eyes and call on them individually to tell about what they remember or liked best about the outdoor experience. If the group is large, you may wish to have two or more Sharing Circles, with an adult leader for each circle.

You may wish to have soft music playing during this quiet time. You may also wish to lead the children in a type of visualization exercise to help them focus on thoughts, feelings, and images relating to the outdoor experience. Following is an example of what you might say during a simple visualization activity.

> "Let's lie very quietly on the floor for a few minutes. Rest your head on your hands and close your eyes. Think about the walk we took in the woods today. See in your mind the row of evergreen trees that were growing along the fence. See the dark green branches against the blue sky. Hear the birds that were singing as we walked by. Use your imagination and think about rubbing your hand along the bark of the tree. Feel the bumps and ridges on the bark. Now sit down underneath the tree. Lean your back against the trunk of the tree. Feel the strength of the tree supporting your back. Thank the tree for its shade, its beauty, and its strength. Now tell the tree good-by and return with me to the classroom."

After the visualization activity, invite children to talk about their thoughts and feelings. What additional images came to their minds? What thoughts? If the tree could speak to them, what would it say? What would they like to tell the tree?

Experience Stories. As children talk about their experiences and insights following an outdoor experience, you may wish to write down their words and make simple pencil drawings based on what they say.

In addition to simple line drawings, actual objects (e.g. seeds, leaves, twigs, etc.) can be attached to the experience story page. These objects are glued or taped to the paper and should come from what the children have found or suggested for inclusion in their story. This concept is illustrated in the story presented on page 119.

In addition to open-ended experience stories, pre-formatted journal entries might also be used. Such journals might be in the form of group versus individual journals and formatted in "big-book" style. "Big Books" are very large books (usually about 14 inches by 17 inches in size).

See page 121 for an example of a page from a pre-formatted journal.

While such pages can be made "Big Book" size, they could also be formatted for storage in a 3-ring binder. One advantage of using a 3-ring binder is that the finished product can then become part of the classroom library or book corner and even sent home to share with the parents.

Where to Go

The best places to go to learn about the natural environment are those places which are close, fairly easy to get to, and offer variety and interest. To be avoided are places that are overwhelming in terms of physical arrangements (e.g., transportation, safety concerns, etc.). If the purpose of the trip is to learn about nature, other places to be avoided include places that offer more of an artificial, or people-made, environment than a **natural** environment. Such places include amusement parks and playgrounds featuring more equipment than grounds. Places offering interest and variety in regard to learning about the natural environment include a vegetable garden, a woods, a stream, a tomato field, etc. Additional ideas on where to go and what to look for are presented in the following sections.

Part II: Implementing the Curriculum

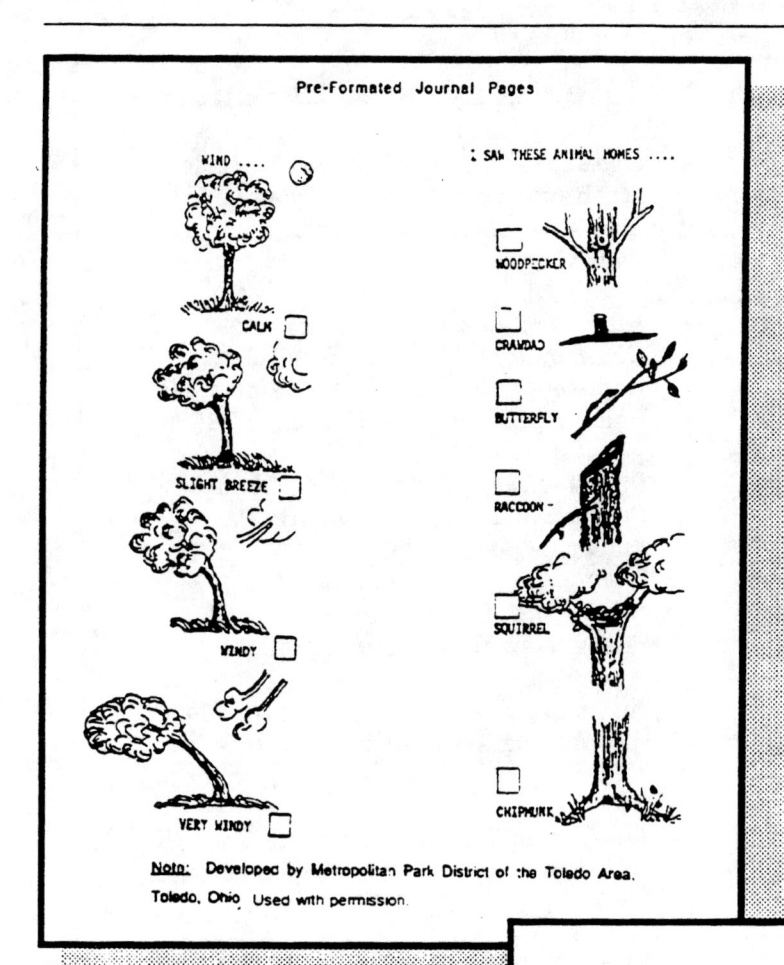

Pre-Formated Journal Pages

WIND ....
- CALM
- SLIGHT BREEZE
- WINDY
- VERY WINDY

I SAW THESE ANIMAL HOMES ....
- WOODPECKER
- CRAWDAD
- BUTTERFLY
- RACCOON
- SQUIRREL
- CHIPMUNK

Note: Developed by Metropolitan Park District of the Toledo Area, Toledo, Ohio. Used with permission.

Experience Story with Real Objects

Today we went to a woods. We found pieces of bark and floated them on the water. There were lots of trees by the pond.

real bark

119

Suggested Children's Books

Long, Earlene. *GONE FISHING.* Illustrations by Richard Brown. Houghton, 1984. 32 pages. Fiction. Interest Level: Ages 2-5.

Stock, Catherine. *SOPHIE'S KNAPSACK.* Illustrations by author. Lothrop, 1988. Fiction. Interest Level: Ages 3-7.

Florian, Douglas. *NATURE WALK.* Illustrations by author. Greenwillow, 1989. Fiction. Interest Level: Ages 2-6.

McMillan, Bruce. *COUNTING WILDFLOWERS.* Illustrations by author. Lothrop, 1986. Nonfiction. Interest Level: Ages 2-5.

Showers, Paul. *THE LISTENING WALK.* Illustrations by Aliki. Harper, 1991. Fiction. Interest Level: Ages 3-6.

Ziefert, Harriet. *SARAH'S QUESTIONS.* Illustrations by Susan Bonners. Lothrop, 1986. Fiction. Interest Level: Ages 4-6.

Tafuri, Nancy. *DO NOT DISTURB.* Illustrations by author. Greenwillow, 1987. Fiction. Interest Level: Ages 2-7.

Recommended Resources

Open the Door, Let's Explore. R. Redleaf, Mt. Rainier, MD: Gryphon House, 1983. Chapter 2. The World of Wonderful Walks.

Hug a Tree and Other Things to do Outdoors with Young Children. R. Rockwell, E. Sherwood, R. Williams. Mt. Rainier, MD: Gryphon House, Inc. 1986.

Investigating Nature through Outdoor Projects. V. Brown. Harrisburg, PA: Stackpole Books, 1983.

Nature With Children of all Ages. E. Sisson. New York: Prentice Hall, 1982.

Talking to Fireflies, Shrinking the Moon. E. Duensing. New York: Penguin Books, 1990.

The Outside Play and Learning Book. K. Miller. Mt. Rainier, MD: Gryphon House, 1989.

Earth Child. K. Sheehan, & M. Waidner. Tulsa, OK: Council Oak Books, 1991. Chapter 1. The Circle of Day and Night.

Nature Activities for Early Childhood. J. Nickelsburg. Menlo Park, CA: Addison-Wesley Publishing Co., 1976.

Wildlife in the City

When asked where to go to find wildlife, many people answer "in the zoo," "in Africa," or "in the woods." Not many people think of the variety of wildlife living in the city. If they do think of animals (other than pets) that live in the city, they usually think in terms of pests versus sources of enjoyment. Yet, once we learn to accept and appreciate them, the animals in the city can teach us many things about the natural world and be a source of wonder and enjoyment.

There are many different kinds of wildlife living in and around the busiest cities. There are squirrels, birds, chipmunks, opossums, toads, bats, snails, garter snakes, bumblebees, butterflies, crickets, ants, ladybugs, spiders, earthworms, raccoons, and a wide variety of insects. While certain types of wildlife can pose health problems—if where they live is too close to (or inside of!) the homes and yards of humans—there are ways to live in harmony with many of the different forms of wildlife sharing the city environment with us.

Community resources. To learn more about wildlife in the city, certain community resources should not be overlooked. These might include a zoo, nature center, and the city parks. Zoos and nature centers often have educational specialists who would be happy to meet with the children to discuss the behavior and characteristics of animals. Sometimes a visit from a "traveling zoo" can also be arranged. Many parks and nature centers have naturalists who offer programs for children of all ages. Some communities also have science centers and aquariums. Not to be overlooked are the public libraries and art museums—both of which may offer special programs or exhibits about wildlife.

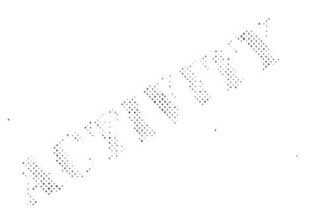

Wildlife Hunt

Background information: To help children become aware of the different types of wildlife in the city, you might go on a wildlife hunt. The purpose of the "hunt" is not to harm or capture any of the animals, but to grow in understanding and appreciation of the different types of wildlife and how they live. If the wildlife hunt extends beyond the school yard, it's important to have the help of at least several other adults. These adults should understand and be sympathetic with the purpose of the activity. There should be one adult for each group of two or three children.

Procedures:
1. Explain the purpose of the wildlife hunt to the children and the adults.
2. Tell the children and adults to look for wildlife and signs of wildlife. Caution them not to touch any of the animals and not to disturb their habitat.
3. Remind the adults that their role is to look after the children's safety and show interest in the children's explorations.
4. Encourage the adults to take field notes about their findings. Let them know that it's not important to write down the names of the different animals nor facts about how they live. Tell them to record what the children say.
5. After a specified amount of time, everyone meets at an agreed-upon location.
6. Each small group and/or each child is given an opportunity to share with the larger group what they found.

Suggestions:
- Talk to children in advance about the process of taking field notes. Share with them some examples of field notes.

"Bird nest on the ground near a bush. Broken egg shells near the nest. No sign of birds."

"Hole in the ground not far from the creek. Mud built up around the hole. No sign of an animal nearby."

"Rustling sounds in the leaves. Something moved—looked like a small furry animal."

Share some examples of field notes from the writings of different naturalists. Share some interesting information about their life, as well.

Follow-up:
- Add drawings to the field notes.
- Bind the pages into a book format.
- Add this book to the classroom library.

Example: Henry David Thoreau

Henry David loved the world of nature and wanted to live close to nature. He built a log cabin in a woods by Walden Pond. He lived there by himself for two years. During that time, he spent many hours walking through the woods and studying the plants and animals that lived there. He wrote in his journal almost everyday about the things that he saw.

Some of the things he wrote:

".... in September or October, Walden is a perfect forest mirror."

"Each pine is like a great green feather stuck in the ground."

"... the squirrels live in or about every forest tree, or hollow log, and every wall and heap of stones."

"The bluebird carries the sky on his back."

Recommended Resources

Beastly Neighbors. M. Rights. Boston, MA: Little, Brown & Co., 1981.

City Safaris. C. Shaffer, & E. Fielder. San Francisco, CA: Sierra Club Books, 1987.

Environmental Education in the Urban Setting: Rationale and Teaching Activities. H. Coon, & M.L. Bowman. Columbus, OH: ERIC Clearinghouse for Science, Mathematics, and Environmental Education, 1976.

Living Lightly in the City: An Urban Environmental Education Curriculum Guide. M. O'Connor. Milwaukee, WI: Schlitz Audubon Center, 1990.

Adopt An Animal

Background information: Young children may enjoy "adopting" an animal living near the school or in the school yard. Because the animal they're adopting is a wild animal, it's important to help the children understand that the animal is not a pet and that they do not have to "take care of" the animal unless it is in danger. For this activity, the purpose of "adopting" is to get to know the animal better.

Procedures:
1. Look for animals in or near the school yard. See if they stay there or return over time.
2. Encourage the children to spend time observing the animal, noting its physical characteristics and its behavior.
3. Share books about the animal.
4. Take pictures of the animal or even video tape its activity, if possible.

Suggestions:
- Alert the groundskeeper about the presence of the animal. Engage his or her assistance in protecting the animal and its habitat.

Follow-up:
- Write some information about the animal in the parent newsletter. Encourage the parents to share information about any animals in or around their yard. Children could bring in pictures of these animals for show-and-tell.

Learning that Plants Are Wildlife, Too

Background information: Everything in the natural world is connected. Plants play a very important role in the web of existence. In fact, most animals would not be able to live in the city unless they had access to plants. Thus, getting to know wildlife in the city should include an awareness and appreciation of the many different types of plants found in the city. These plants may be growing in the cracks of the sidewalk, flourishing in neighborhood yards, or growing in empty lots. Trees and flowers often grace the city parks and sides of streets. Many changes can be observed over time by becoming aware of the plants that live in and around the city. Children can be encouraged to notice and enjoy these changes, both in the many different plants that grow "on their own" and the more "domesticated" plants that grow in gardens and flower beds.

Procedures:
1. While still indoors, ask the children to guess how many different kinds of plants they could find in the school yard.
2. Give them each a "cardboard window" (i.e., a cardboard frame about 10 by 12 inches).
3. Take the "windows" outside and lay them on a non-paved section of the ground.
4. Ask the children to look carefully in their windows. How many children can see more than one kind of plant in their window?
5. Move the windows to another place in the yard. Can they see any different kinds of plants?

Suggestions:
- Give each child a magnifying glass. Encourage them to use it when looking through their windows.
- Encourage the children to look for small animals as well as different kinds of plants. Do the plants seem to help the animals in any way (e.g., as food, protection, place to live, etc.)?

Follow-up:
- Draw a window on a blank sheet of paper. Encourage the children to fill in things they might see when they look through the window.

Wildlife in the Country

The country, or rural communities, feature a wide variety of plants and animals. Interesting places to visit to learn about these plants and animals include a farm, an apple orchard, a pumpkin patch, a woods, a meadow, and a lake.

Lake, pond, or stream. Go to a lake, pond, or stream. Dip out a small amount of water. Pour the water into a shallow pan. Use a large magnifying glass to look at the water. Encourage the children to talk about the many different things they see. What does it look like? Does it move? Do you think it's living? How big is it, etc.?

Other things to look for while near a lake, pond, or stream are small stones, shells, and snail trails. You might also look for little holes in the ground and animal foot prints in the sand. The holes may have been dug by crayfish and the variety of animal tracks may indicate a number of different types of animals living nearby.

While there are many things to see in and near a body of water, there are also interesting sounds to listen for. If you walk quietly along the edge, you may hear the splish, splash, and plop of frogs jumping in the water. You may hear the sound of water trickling over rocks, birds singing nearby, and the sound of wind in the trees and grasses.

Woods. While living trees seem to dominate the landscape in a wooded area, there are many other things to look for. Children can be encouraged to see, not just the trees, but the spaces between the trees. Are the trees growing close together? Are they touching each other? Look up at the canopy of leaves and branches. Which trees reach out the furthest—the ones that grow close to each other or the ones that are farther apart? After the children discover that the trees with branches spreading the furthest are the ones that aren't growing close to each other, they may ask why. Before suggesting the answer to this or any other question, encourage the children to venture answers of their own. Always praise the children for offering their ideas, and build your response on what they have suggested.

The leaves on the trees need sunlight. If trees are growing close to each other, their branches tend to reach toward the sun. On the other hand, if there is a lot of empty space around the tree, it can spread its branches wide and still get the sun it needs. After you talk about this concept with the children, suggest that the children pretend to be trees. Have one group stand close to each other and reach their arms toward the sun. Have another group disperse over a larger area and spread their branches out versus up.

One of the most interesting things to look for in a wooded area is a decaying tree. While some children may not recognize its beauty at first, a closer look will often intrigue everyone in the group. Are there new plants growing up out of the decaying log? Does it look like the decaying log is becoming a part of the forest floor?

After the children have had time to explore the decaying tree through their senses of sight, feel, and smell, you might invite volunteers to take turns lying down beside the fallen tree. Encourage them to think of themselves as the decaying tree. How does it feel? Is it cool and restful? Do you feel like you're becoming a part of the floor in the woods? Do you feel like you've lived a long time and now it's time to make room for the baby trees to grow?

A woods is also home to many small animals. The children might see some of these animals; others they may only hear. Encourage the children to be very quiet and listen for sounds of animals. The first thing they usually hear is the singing of birds. Sometimes, they'll hear the pecking of a woodpecker or the buzzing of a fly or bee. If they're patient and quiet, they may also hear the sound of chipmunks or squirrels moving through the leaves.

Encourage the children to look for signs of where the animals live. During the fall and winter, they may find empty bird nests. They may also see squirrel nests in the branches of the trees. A round hole in the trunk of a tree may be home to a woodpecker and an opening at the base of the tree may be where a chipmunk lives.

Meadow or Open field. A walk across a meadow or open field can lead to a variety of nature-related adventures. Many different creatures live in fields—ants, grasshoppers, rabbits, snakes, mice, a variety of birds, and woodchucks.

Perhaps a nearby farmer or other land owner would be delighted to share the secrets of a field with a group of young children. You might even ask advice about what to look for and what you need to be aware of. Does the farmer know of any unusual tree or wildflower growing in the field? Is he or she aware of poison ivy or a bees' nest? Must you remember to close gates or watch out for crops growing in the field?

As you walk across the field, many kinds of wildlife will hop, fly, or run away when you come near. They're constantly on the lookout for predators, and will think that you're a potential predator, too.

Look carefully at the open, sandy spots for animal tracks. Compare tracks. Can you tell which ones were made by four-legged animals; which by two-legged ones?

At times, get down on your hands and knees. What living things, or evidence of living things, can you find? Do you see any tiny insects or spiders? You may see the white, foamy nest of the spittlebug on a blade of grass or a cocoon attached to a twig.

Look for holes in the ground. Many of them are entrances to underground burrows made and inhabited by small animals—mice, moles, ground squirrels, woodchucks, etc.

Pick up a stone or a piece of wood that has been lying on the ground for awhile. Underneath, you may find white grubs, ant eggs, or centipedes. Dig into the moist soil where you're likely to find earthworms. Return the stone or piece of wood to protect the creatures living there.

On a spring or early summer hike, you may find a field bird's nest. These are usually in a little hollow on the ground or in the middle of a clump of grass. Be careful not to disturb the nest in any way—even touching the eggs may cause the parent bird to desert the nest.

An underground home for people. Do you know of anyone in your area who has an underground home? If so, most young children will be fascinated by the concept and will want to know how it looks and how it feels. On a trip to one such home, children were delighted to learn that the family's garden was on the roof. Strawberries were ripe and, yes, all the children got to pick and eat some of the berries. When they got back to school, they all wanted to draw a picture of a house with strawberries on the roof. They also role played living in an underground home and talked about building underground homes while playing at the sand table. Some water added to the sand and small boxes with cut-out doors allowed children to experiment with constructing their own models of underground homes.

What to Do

While outdoor excursions should always allow a great deal of time for open-ended and unplanned experiences, some pre-planned activities can also enhance the learning experience. Following are a few suggestions of the types of activities that might be included while on an outdoor excursion in the country.

Look for signs of animals. Animals in the wild aren't always easy to observe. The way they camouflage and the way they hide make direct observation of wild animals somewhat difficult— especially for young children who tend to move around a lot and who find waiting quietly extremely difficult. Young children can still use their observational skills to learn a lot about animals in the wild. They can study the many different clues to animal activity. These clues—or signs of animal activity—are usually easier to find than the animals themselves.

Children can work in pairs to look for signs of animals in a specified area. At first, they can be guided to look for one type of clue at a time—these might include animal tracks on the ground, homes for the animals on or near a tree, food leftovers on or near the ground (e.g., nuts opened by rodents, leaves chewed by deer or rabbits, etc.), and sounds of animals in the area.

The following information may help in guiding (not telling!) children in their efforts to discover signs of animals in the country.

- Animal tracks are often found in mud, by shores, or in puddles. Animal tracks are also easy to find in snow and wet sand.
- Animal homes are built in trees as well as on and in the ground. Squirrels and many different birds make nests in trees; other animals use holes in trees for their home. Some animals live under logs and rocks. Many animals make burrows or tunnels in the ground—these include chipmunks, gophers, foxes, and mice. Worms, crayfish, and

snakes also make burrows in the ground or sand.
- Food leftovers can include plant or animal food substances. Leftovers from carnivores (i.e., animal-eaters) include bones, animal fur, or feathers. Plant leftovers include bark gnawed by rodents, pieces of evergreen cones dropped by squirrels, and twigs or tree branches nibbled by beavers.
- Animal sounds frequently heard in the country include squirrels scolding, rodents gnawing, mice or chipmunks running, birds calling, frogs croaking or jumping in the water, and crickets chirping.

Suggested Children's Books

Rylant, Cynthia. *NIGHT IN THE COUNTRY.* Illustrations by Mary Szilagyi. Bradbury, 1986. Fiction, Interest Level: Ages 3-6.

San Souci, Daniel. *NORTH COUNTRY NIGHT.* Illustrations by author. Doubleday, 1990. Nonfiction. Interest Level: Ages 3-6.

Henkes, Kevin. *GRANDPA AND BO.* Illustration by author. Greenwillow, 1986. Fiction. Interest Level: Ages 4-7.

Johnson, Herschel. *A VISIT TO THE COUNTRY.* Illustrations by Romare Bearden. Harper, 1989. Fiction. Interest Level: Ages 4-8.

Collect Animal Tracks

Background information: Plaster casts of animal tracks are easy to make and can help children appreciate the wonder and diversity of the animal kingdom.

Procedures:
1. Collect the necessary materials: the bottom part of a half-gallon milk carton (or other similar container), plaster of Paris, water, mixing stick or spoon, four strips of cardboard about three inches long.
2. Go outdoors with the materials and find a clear animal track.
3. Use the strips of cardboard to build a four-sided barrier around the animal track.
4. Mix the plaster of Paris and water in the milk-carton container. The mixture should be the consistency of a thick soup.
5. Pour the mixture onto the track (inside the barrier).
6. Leave the mixture to harden. This usually takes at least 30 minutes.
7. Remove and rinse the plaster to find a print of the animal track.

Suggestions:
- Display pictures and books of animals and animal tracks.
- While waiting for the mixture to harden, try following the animal tracks as far as you can. Talk about the "story" behind the tracks—What do you think the animal was doing? Where do you think it was going?

Follow-up:
- Collect a set of rubber stamps featuring different animals, animal tracks, and a variety of habitats (trees, grasses, pond, etc.). Encourage children to make up stories about the animals as they play with the stamps.

Enjoying Nature in Your Own Back Yard

Implementation Guideline # 11: Introduce children to wildlife and other aspects of nature in and around the school yard.

Playground Alternatives

When young children go outside at school, they often go to a playground—that is, a place equipped with playground equipment and often featuring walkways over which they ride their bikes and pull their wagons. Such a playground may also feature a sandbox and a grassy area where children might play ball. Not many schools offer a more natural area where children can learn about plants and animals in a natural habitat. Many people might think that when given a choice between two different settings—one featuring swings and slides and the other trees, sand, dirt, and water—that most young children would choose the more traditionally-equipped playground. Such, however, is not the case. According to studies done by Schicker (1988), children prefer outdoor places that allow personal investigation and manipulation of materials over school playgrounds. They "love a certain amount of untidiness and prefer 'undesigned' and 'ungroomed' areas for play" (Schicker, 1988, p. 15). Their favorite places were located near water, bicycle paths, or in sports fields. Following are some of the suggestions offered by Schicker on how to enhance children's exposure to wildlife.

1. Plan an area of the yard where you do nothing at all—that is, where you allow native plants to flourish. This means avoiding the use of machines (including mowers), fertilizers, herbicides, pruning, mulching and spraying. This becomes the "nature area" and should be valued as such, versus looked upon as wasted space.
2. Construct a wildlife observation and feeding station. Invite wildlife to the area by providing feeders, birdbaths, scratch and dust areas, birdhouses, gravel, sand, hollow logs, brush and rock piles.
3. Build tree houses and encourage tree climbing. Before constructing

a tree house, however, several things must be kept in mind, including child safety and tree protection. According to Schicker (1988), trees need to be old and strong enough to support a treehouse. They should have a six-inch diameter at breast height and should be eight to fifteen feet tall. The tree house should be constructed in a way that does not put the entire load of support on the tree. Sturdy poles sunk into the ground can help support the weight of the structure. Pounding nails into the tree should be avoided, as punctures into the bark can damage the tree. The tree house should be constructed on the lower branches of the tree. A bed of sand at the base of the tree can be added as a safety feature.

4. Set aside a portion of the school yard as an adventure playground. The idea behind adventure playgrounds is freedom on the part of the children to manipulate and move natural materials. Such materials could include piles of leaves, sand, dirt, tree limbs and stumps, gravel, rocks, pine cones, shells, etc. Digging and raking tools should be provided, as should buckets, bags, sprinkling cans, and a small wheelbarrow, if possible. Adventure playgrounds should be dynamic and flexible versus static. They should allow for and invite exploration and initiative on the part of the children.

Inviting Wildlife to Your Yard

Feeding the birds and providing habitats. There are a number of different ways to invite wildlife to your own back yard. Setting up a bird feeder is one of the simpler ways to attract birds to where you can easily watch them. With a little ingenuity, bird feeders can be made from plastic bottles, milk cartons, coconut shells, and mesh bags. Hang the feeders outside the classroom windows for easy observation.

For a special observational treat, try attracting hummingbirds during the spring and summer months. Most pet food stores have hummingbird feeders and suggestions on how to attract these unusual birds.

Certain plants serve as natural bird feeders. Berry-producing bushes and trees provide both food and shelter. Marigolds and zinnias produce seeds that are eaten by finches and sparrows. Other brightly-colored flowers, such as red and orange impatiens, attract hummingbirds.

Providing suitable habitats for birds is also an effective and environmentally friendly way of inviting them into your back yard. Birds build their homes in trees, bushes, and brush piles. Different types of birds will also move into birdhouses. Easy-to-attract birds include the bluebird, chickadee, purple martin, robin, tufted titmouse, woodpecker, and wren. Simple birdhouses can be purchased or made. Specifications for building birdhouses are often available through craft shops and wildlife stores.

Bird baths also attract a variety of birds and provide, not only a source of needed water for the birds, but also an interesting and enjoyable way to watch the birds. Bird baths should be shallow and easy to clean. Fresh water should be added everyday during the summer, and frequent cleaning is a must.

Another way to encourage birds to stay nearby is to provide a variety of materials that birds might use in building their nests. This activity should be done early in spring. Materials for the nests could include pieces of yarn, lint from the dryer, and very narrow strips of cloth.

Invite a toad to the yard. Toads may take up residence in the yard, if provided a place to live, with proper food, shelter, and water. Toads eat bugs and will thus serve as an asset for your gardening efforts. You can meet the toad's shelter and water needs through something as simple as two small plastic food containers (e.g., margarine tubs, cottage cheese containers, etc.).

One container becomes the toad's swimming pool. Dig a hole in the ground, big enough to hold the tub. Insert the tub, pack the dirt around it to hold it in place, and then fill it with water. Check several times a week to see that there is enough water.

Cut a doorway out of the top edge of the other container. The doorway should be big enough for the toad to fit through. Then turn the container upside down, near the pool of water. You may wish to weight it down in some way, so that the wind will not blow it away. You can make it an underground home, by piling dirt over and around it; or you can place a small rock on the top, with instructions to the children (and grounds caretaker!) to not disturb. It's best to locate the toad's home close to the garden, if you have one, and out of the way of busy play areas.

Establish a butterfly meadow. For inviting wildlife to your yard, a butterfly meadow could also be established. This requires a place to lay eggs, food plants for the caterpillars, a place to form cocoons, and nectar sources for the adult butterflies. Pesticides should be avoided entirely, as butterflies will not survive well if any are present. Butterfly meadows require a great deal of direct sunlight (six to ten hours daily) to support growth of the plants required. While butterflies feed on nectar from flowers, the caterpillars eat the leafy vegetation of specific plants. Butterflies prefer flowers that are bright in color— red, orange, yellow, purple, and pink. Some of their favorite flowers are milkweed, clover, dwarf marigolds, lilacs, phlox, zinnias, thyme, common daylily, asters, and goldenrod. Some of these may grow on their own in the "nature area" of the yard, while others may be planted in a flower garden. It's best to plant masses of nectar-producing flowers in full sunlight beds.

You might also look for butterfly feeders and hibernation boxes at nature stores. Butterfly feeders are usually designed to feed either nectar or rotting fruit to butterflies. The hibernation boxes provide overwintering butterflies a suitable place to spend the winter. It's usually recommended that these boxes be filled with long strips of bark for clinging surfaces for adult butterflies and that they be placed in a shady area.

Recommended Resource

Contact the National Wildlife Federation for information on their schoolyard habitat program. 8925 Leesburg Pike, Vienna, VA 22180.

Playing Games

Certain games in the school yard can enhance children's understanding and appreciation of the natural world. Many such games are outlined in Joseph Cornell's books, *Sharing Nature With Children* (1979) and *Sharing the Joy of Nature* (1989). Additional suggestions are offered below.

Ants' Eye View. Children are encouraged to think of themselves as being as small as an ant and living in the grass. They then lie down in the grass and try to see the world as the ant would see it. If they were an ant, how big would a blade of grass seem to them? How far away would the sky be? Where would they hide if a lawn mower came?

Treasure Hunt. Needed for the game of Treasure Hunt are laminated pictures of objects from the natural world (e.g., a pebble, acorn, leaf, twig, dandelion, bird, pine cone, etc.). Children are asked to work in pairs and to find the real objects that match their pictures. They are asked to observe their item very carefully—to find out how it feels, smells, sounds, etc. After a period of time, everyone is called to a sharing circle. Here, they take turns showing their pictures, telling where they found their item, and what they observed about it.

Dramatic play. Dramatic play need not be confined to inside the classroom. Given the right props, nature-related dramatic play can flourish in the school yard. Set up a tent and watch the "campers" move into action. Provide a spot to dig and some digging tools and you'll have a garden in the making. Sticks and dried leaves make wonderful "plants." Acorns, winged maple tree seeds, and kernels of corn make planting seeds quite realistic. A sprinkling can adds to the fun.

Washable stuffed animals can go outdoors, where children can then look for places for the animals to live — the bunny under the bushes, the monkey in the tree, the bear in a den, etc. Or provide simple props inviting the children to take on the role of different animals. Watch the "animals" find their own places to live, food to eat, and noises to make.

Hide and Seek. This game teaches the children about camouflage. Have laminated pictures of familiar animals. The pictures should be at least the size of your hand, so that they won't be too difficult to find. The pictures should be the natural color of the animal. Then, while all the children close their eyes, hide one animal at a time in a place where the color of the surroundings will make the animal hard to find (e.g., place a green grasshopper in the grass, a brown rabbit in some dried leaves, etc.). While the children still have their eyes closed, you might give them some verbal clues as to what animal is hiding (e.g., "This animal is about the size of a football. It is brown and has a tail. It wiggles its nose and likes to eat food out of the garden."). After someone guesses what it is (a rabbit), the children then look for the animal. The children can take turns hiding the other animals and, if they can, give verbal clues as to what animal is hiding.

Another version of the hiding game focuses on "worms." Each child is given a pipe cleaner worm. Their task is to find suitable cover to protect the worm from its predators. Of course, some colors are easily found while others blend in with their surroundings.

You might also take the pipe cleaner worms and scatter them over a grassy area. Children are to find as many as they can. Which ones do they find first?

The Mystery Eater. The Mystery Eater is played by putting out food for the animals and then trying to figure out who ate it. Food—such as bits of dog food or cat food, small pieces of fruit, or bread crumbs—are spread outside on a flat, bare surface. Flour is then sprinkled lightly on the ground around the food. After an hour or so—or maybe the next day—check to see if the food has been eaten. Study any prints left behind in the flour and try to identify the mystery eater.

Leading the Blind. For this game, each child is paired with a partner. Partners take turns being blindfolded. The child who is not blindfolded guides his or her partner through the yard and helps the partner experience plants and other things in the yard through the senses of touch, sound, and smell. The "blind" person then talks about what it is he or she is experiencing and tries to guess what it is (e.g., leaf, pine cone, stick, seed, stone, flower, etc.).

Lily Pad Jump. Place carpet squares on the ground to represent lily pads. Invite the children to jump like frogs from pad to pad.

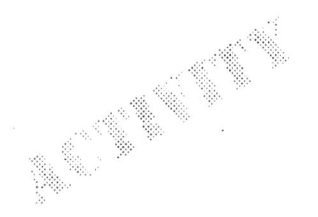

Start a Compost Pile

Background information: The magic of composting will not only impress the children but will also provide a rich fertilizer for your garden. Compost piles are simple collections of plant and animal materials piled up enough to decompose. Decomposition happens through a natural heating process and the work of tiny organisms. Compost can be made in bins of wood, concrete blocks, chicken wire, or other similar materials. Even an old garbage can would work well. Holes must be punched in the garbage can, as all compost bins need openings for air circulation. A compost area need not be large, but should be at least 3 feet by 3 feet with a height of about 3 feet.

Procedures:
1. Build a compost cake. Start by loosening the soil where the bin will sit. This is necessary to allow for good drainage.
2. Make a bottom layer of dry materials about 4-8 inches deep. Chop large materials so that they will decompose faster.
3. Add a layer of green vegetation and kitchen scraps This layer should also be 4-8 inches deep.
4. Add soil, about 1 inch deep, to make a top layer.
5. Your compost bin is now ready, and you can begin adding other compost materials. Materials that can be used in a compost bin include grass clippings, food scraps (except meat, bones, or fat), manure, and leaves. Almost anything that was once alive can be used for compost.

Suggestions:
- Inform parents of this activity so that they will understand children's comments about throwing things in a scrap pile. Invite them to visit the compost pile.
- Explore the process of decomposition in the classroom. Fill a plastic bag with some "once living" materials (e.g., food scraps, grass clippings, etc.). Observe what happens over a period of time.

Follow-up:
- Set up a worm bin in the classroom.
- Look for examples of decomposition outdoors (under piles of leaves, around fallen trees, etc.).

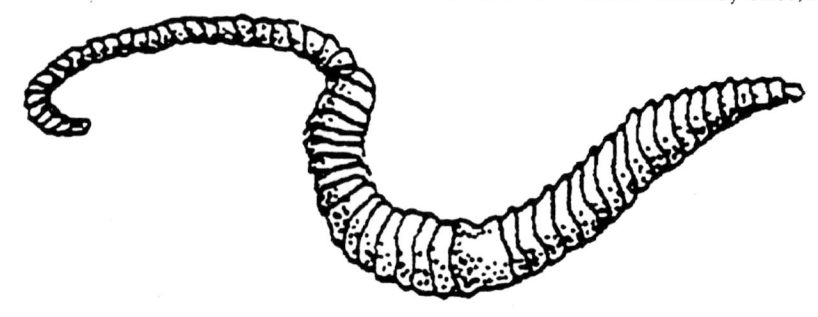

Additional Suggestions

1. Use railroad ties or another similar material for enclosing a large rectangular-shaped sand box. Children can sit on the railroad ties and also use them as shelves. During the winter, cover the sand with plastic and flood the sandbox area with water. In this way, you'll have an ice skating rink.
2. To help children gain some early concepts about wind and weather, you might attach a large wind sock to the top of the flag pole and mount a large thermometer on the side of one of the buildings. You could also supply a number of pinwheels, both as yard decorations and for the children to play with. The use of soap bubbles and kites are other enjoyable ways for children to experience the effect of wind.
3. Use a variety of ground covers for the children to experience and explore. These could include grass, gravel, sand, wood chips, and plants of various kinds.
4. Plant a garden. Include flowers for picking, vegetables of all kinds, and some herbs. In making your choice about the type of vegetables to plant, consider variety in how the plants grow and produce food. Include plants with vines (melons, pumpkins), stalks (pop corn, sweet corn), and tubers (potatoes, radishes, carrots). Also include plants providing rich sensory stimulation in the areas of sight, sound, touch, smell, and taste. Brightly-colored flowers can be used to stimulate the sense of sight. Japanese lanterns and money plants that rattle after they're dried can be used for sound. The sense of touch can be stimulated through such plants as the hard-leafed yucca plant and the soft lambs ear. Roses and marigolds stimulate the sense of smell, while strawberries and a variety of spices can stimulate the sense of taste.

   If space is limited, you might try gardening in containers. In addition to saving space, container gardens also offer several other advantages. Container gardening can be inexpensive, in that many suitable containers are free. These include tires, baskets, crates, buckets, plastic pails, bleach jugs, and cement blocks.

   Containers also have the advantage of being movable. You may wish to move containers to where they can get more sun, or move them inside at night to protect them from vandalism. You may also wish to send them home with children for nurturing over a long school break or as gifts for their parents.

   Another advantage of container gardening is the fact that it is not overwhelming. You can begin very simply, with only a few small containers.

   Celebrate the planting of your garden with special song and dance. This custom, already in place in some countries, can make planting a garden a memorable event.
5. Use paint brushes to "paint" sidewalks and the sides of buildings. Ice cubes are also fun and interesting to use in painting outdoor pictures.

6. Take magnifiers in the sandbox or near the flower garden. Invite children to describe what they see.
7. Make impressions of bark, leaves, stones, seeds, etc in rolled-out playdough.
8. Decorate large boxes for different outdoor dramatic play themes--e.g. club house, lemonade stand, train engine, boat, etc.
9. Set up an outdoor water table. A large tub placed on top of a low picnic table would work well. Float materials found in the yard-leaves, sticks, small pieces of bark, pine cones, seed, etc.
10. Hold story time outdoors. Try to fit the theme to the setting. Use related outdoor props, whenever possible.
11. Plant a tree. Water it frequently.
12. Set up a tent and watch the fun! Equip with appropriate props-- camp cookware, firewood, etc.
13. Spray a spider web. Fill a small plant sprayer with water. Go outside and look for spider webs. Carefully spray the web with fine mist. The water will make the web more visible and enhance the children's appreciation of its beauty.
14. Make the outdoor learning environment a place of beauty and variety. Plant different types of trees and bushes; have flowers blooming from early spring (crocuses, hyacinths, and tulips) until late fall (pansies, petunias, and snapdragons); make rocks and logs a part of the landscape; and invite birds, rabbbits, and squirrels to frequent the yard.
15. Establish a "listening place" outdoors. This should be a quiet place to sit, either as a group or individually, to listen to the sounds of nature.

Resources for Gardening

Children's Gardens: A Field Guide for Teachers, Parents, and Volunteers by Bremner and Pusey (1982). Common Ground Program, 21615 South Grand Avenue, Room 400, Los Angeles, CA 90007.

Growing Up Green. Hickaby & Skelsey, 1978. Workman Publishing Company.

A Book of Vegetables by Harriet L. Sobol

Corn is Maize: The Gift of Indians by Aliki

Eat the Fruit, Plant the Seed by Millicent Selsan

In My Garden: A Child's Gardening Book by Helen and Kelly Oechsli

The Kids Garden Book by Petrich & Dalton

Mr. Plum's Paradise by Elisa Trimby

My Garden, A Journal for Gardening Throughout the Year by L. Murphy

The Pumpkin People by David & Maggie Cavagnaro
The Reason for a Flower by Ruth Heller

Suggested Children's Books

Hughes, Shirley. *OUT AND ABOUT*. Illustrations by author. Lothrop, 1988. Fiction. Interest Level: Ages 2-6.

Ryder, Joanne. *STEP INTO THE NIGHT*. Illustrations by Dennis Nolan. Macmillan, 1988. Fiction. Interest Level: Ages 4-8.

Denslow, Sharon Phillips. *NIGHT OWLS*. Illustrations by Jill Kastner. Bradbury, 1990. Fiction Interest Level: Ages 4-7.

Otto, Carolyn, *THAT SKY, THAT RAIN*. Illustrations by Megan Lloyd. Harper, 1990. Fiction. Interest Level: Ages 3-6.

Ehlert, Lois. *FEATHERS FOR LUNCH*. Illustrations by author. Harcourt, 1990. Fiction. Interest Level: Ages 3-8.

Selsam, Millicent, and Ronald Goor. *BACKYARD INSECTS*. Photos by Ronald Goor. Scholastic, 1988. 40 pages. Nonfiction. Interest Level: Ages 3-8.

Carrick, Donald. *THE TREE*. Illustrations by author. Macmillan, 1971. Fiction. Interest Level: Ages 3-8.

Pederson, Judy. *THE TINY PATIENT*. Illustrations by author. Knopf, 1989. Fiction. Interest Level: Ages 3-6.

Udry, Janice May. *A TREE IS NICE*. Illustrations by Marc Simont. Harper, 1956. Fiction. Interest Level: Ages 3-8.

Lavies, Bianca. *TREE TRUNK TRAFFIC*. Photos by author. Dutton, 1989. Nonfiction. Interest Level: Ages 4-8.

Recommended Resources

Beyond the Classroom: Exploration of Schoolground and Backyard. C. Roth, C. Cervoni, T. Wellnitz, & E. Arms. Lincoln, MA: Massachusetts Audubon Society, 1988.

Earth Child. K. Sheehan, & M. Waidner. Tulsa, OK: Council Oak Books, 1991. Chapter 4. Trees are Terrific

My Recipes are for the Birds. I. Cosgrove. New York: Doubleday, 1976.

Outdoor Areas as Learning Laboratories. A. McCormack. Columbus, OH: ERIC Clearinghouse for Science, Mathematics, and Environmental Education, 1979.

Part III

Special Considerations

"There was a child went forth every day, And the first object he looked upon, that object he became."

Walt Whitman

"Teaching a child not to step on a caterpillar is as valuable to the child as it is to the caterpillar."

Bradley Miller

Chapter 6
Individualizing the Program
Special Needs and Interests

Implementation Guideline #12: Individualize the program to meet special needs and interests.

Dealing With Fears

Many children (and adults) fear some things in nature. These might be spiders, bats, snakes, or thunder. The child's fear—and your own—should be recognized, not denied. Accurate information in a nonthreatening environment will often help dispel a fear. The important thing to remember is that fears are real and are not overcome by ridicule or embarrassment or by forcing a child to do something that is uncomfortable for him or her.

Be sensitive to the children's feelings and anxieties. It's helpful to talk to individual children about their feelings and gradually lead them to a better understanding of that which they are afraid. Better understandings usually lead to more relaxed feelings and deeper appreciations.

Be honest and open about your own feelings, as well. If you're afraid of snakes or spiders, or if you love the smell of lilacs, share these feelings with the children. In the case of being afraid of certain animals, you can admit your fear to the children, while at the same time, conveying a sense of respect for the animal. By sharing your feelings with the children, you'll help them to identify and deal with their own emotions.

Remember that animals get frightened, too, and their fears should also be respected. Too much handling, loud sounds, and unexpected movement can all frighten an animal—whether in the classroom or out-of-doors. Respect for the animal should be discussed with the children.

Introducing a variety of animals in the classroom offers rich learning experiences, if the feelings of both the children and the animals are taken into consideration. Wild animals should be kept indoors for no more than one or two weeks and should be chosen very carefully. While it's OK to catch and hold for observation such animals as earthworms and spiders, it's not OK to do so with baby birds and raccoons. When in doubt, check with a naturalist. When wild animals are brought into the classroom, they should be put in as natural a habitat as possible and always returned to the place where they were first collected.

Animals should always be handled with care and respect, and no child should be forced to touch an animal if he or she is frightened by the experience. Some children will need more time and reassurance than others, before they are ready to touch or hold an animal—especially animals with which they are unfamiliar.

Introducing an Animal to the Children

Background information: Many children are afraid of animals, especially of animals with which they are not familiar. When introducing an animal to the children, it's good to do so gradually—moving from indirect to direct contact, from distance to near.

Procedures:
1. Tell that children that you have an animal to introduce to them. Have it in a box or cage at this point.
2. Show them a picture of the animal and talk about some of its characteristics.
3. Tell the children that you'd like to take the animal out of its cage and allow them to hold or pet the animal (if appropriate), but that they do not have to do it if they don't want to.
4. Take the animal out of its cage and hold it in your hand or on your lap. Pet the animal and talk about some of the things the animal does or what it eats.
5. If appropriate, tell the children that you'd like to place the animal on the floor or table top, but first ask them if that is OK. Assure the children that you will not let the animal run over to them.
6. Encourage the children to watch closely to see what the animal does. Give it some food (if appropriate) and watch how the animal eats.
7. Ask the children if any of them would like to touch or pet the animal. Tell them that you will hold the animal while they do so.
8. Ask the children if any of them would like to hold the animal. Show them how to hold it in a respectful and caring way.

Suggestions:
- Invite a naturalist, a veterinarian, or a traveling zoo to visit the classroom with selected animals.
- Show video tapes of animals in their natural habitats.
- Display books and pictures of animals.

Follow-up:
- Encourage the children to imagine what it would feel like to be a certain animal (e.g., How would it feel to be an earthworm?). Encourage them to role play being that animal.
- Provide stuffed animals and puppets of animals. Choose ones that are lifelike versus cartoon characters.

Focus on the Children's Interests

Whether working indoors or outdoors with a group of children, it's important to focus on what is of interest them. Avoid letting your ideas or agenda for the day supersede what the children find of interest. It's attention to what is interesting to the children that will maintain their active involvement in any nature-related experience. If when you have planned a bark-rubbing activity, children find a large mushroom or fungus growing on the tree, let the children feel and talk about the mushroom or fungus. If you run out of time and never get around to the bark-rubbing activity, know that you have sparked an interest in a different aspect of nature. It's the interest in nature that is important, not the finished product of a bark-rubbing to display in the classroom or to take home to parents.

Focusing on what children find of interest often translates into capturing the teachable moment. One such example is presented in the book *Teaching in the Outdoors* by Donald, William, and Elizabeth Hammerman. Their story is about a trip to explore the rock formations around a small lake. One of the first things some of the children observed, however, was a mass of black, jellylike eggs near the edge of the water. Upon close observation, the children discovered that each small egg had a baby tadpole inside. Very carefully, a few of the eggs were transferred to a container filled with lake water and placed in an area where all the children could see what was going to happen. There, before their very eyes, the eggs began to hatch. Tapping into the magic of this teachable moment allowed the children to experience the wonder of birth.

Children with Disabilities

Changes in approach and adaptations to materials are sometimes necessary when working with children with special needs. Some children, because of motor delays or problems may need larger and easier-to-handle tools and utensils. They may also need some help in stabilizing their materials when working with small objects, such as putting a puzzle together, turning the pages in a book, planting seedlings, making a collage, etc. A child with a visual impairment will need more verbal descriptions of what's in the environment and how things in the environment are positioned in relation to him- or herself. The child with a hearing impairment needs more visual cues, including face-to-face communication. A child in a wheelchair needs to have materials brought close to him or her—or be lifted out of the chair and placed in the pile of leaves or field of clover. The child in the wheelchair wants to pet the goat and feel the sheep's wooly coat as much as the other children. He or she should be given the opportunity to do so. Just watching and wishing is not enough. The child in the wheelchair--or the child with any type of disability—learns through hands-on experiences just like all the other children. If there are barriers preventing the child with special needs from interacting with his or her environment, adaptations must be made so that this child, too, can be actively involved in the learning experience.

Recommended Resource
The Wonder of It: Exploring How the World Works, Bonnie Neugebauer (Ed.), Exchange Press, Redmond, Washington. See Section on "Meaning Through Process: Science for Children with Special Needs", pp. 35-38.

Infants and Toddlers

Children are never too young for learning about nature or going on nature outings. There are additional precautions, however, that should be taken when working with infants and toddlers outdoors.

- Choose clothing that will protect the children from the cold, dampness, sunburn, scratches, rashes, stings, and bites. Choose long pants and closed-toe shoes. Unless it's very hot, long sleeve shirts are also recommended.
- Stay within a few yards of the children at all times. Be sure that each child is constantly within sight. For outings beyond an enclosed school yard, there should be one adult for every mobile child under the age of three.
- Don't let the children put anything in their mouths—leaves, stones, berries, etc.
- Keep hands and fingers out of holes. Many holes serve as homes for animals. A startled animal could harm the children.
- Know poison ivy and poison oak and keep the children away from these plants.

Infants and toddlers will need something to do when outdoors. If they can't pick the flowers and leaves, need to stay away from the edge of the pond, and are told not to put their hands inside interesting holes, they'll need some alternatives. Following are some ideas on how to keep the children involved in safe and interesting ways.

- Bring along small stuffed animals or puppets. Take them for a walk, roll with them in the grass, and let them lie on a log.
- Help children discover the feel of things—the softness of the grass, the roughness of the bark, the warmth of sand in the sun, etc. Guide their fingers gently over the surface of things; show them how to bury their hands under the dirt or sand; and lift them high to feel the leaves of the tree brush against their face.
- Take along egg cartons or small plastic bottles. Encourage children to find small things in nature—things they can collect without hurting anything. They might collect blades of grass, feathers, seeds, stones, a handful of earth, etc. Once these items are collected, pour them out on a sidewalk, blanket, or other flat surface. Have the children each choose an item to return it to where it was found.
- Expose the children to a wide variety of sounds, sights, and smells found in nature. Sit beside a stream of water, walk through a woods, and lean against a very big tree.

Recommended Resources

Trails, Tails & Tidepools in Pails, Docents of Nursery Nature Walks, Post Office Box 844, Pacific Palisades, CA 90272, 1992.

Nature For the Very Young. Marcia Bowden, Wiley and Sons.

The Wonder of It: Exploring How the World Works, Bonnie Neugebauer (Ed.), Exchange Press, Redmond, Washington. See Section on "Supporting the Development of a Scientific Mind in Infants and Toddlers", pp. 29-34.

Suggested Children's Books: For Infants and Toddlers

Animal Sounds, by Molly Bang

Good Night Moon, by Margaret Wise Brown

Home for Bunny, by Margaret Wise Brown

Runaway Bunny, by Margaret Wise Brown

Big Animals, by Sara Lynn

Garden Animals, by Sara Lynn

Listen to the City, by Virginia Pellergino

Listen to the Country, by Virginia Pellergino

Involving Families

Implementation Guideline # 13: Invite parent participation in nature-related activities.

All parents have information, feelings, and values about the natural world which can be shared with their children. Such a sharing offers benefits to both the children and their parents.

Benefits

The interest and involvement of parents in nature-appreciation activities intensifies the interest of their children in knowing about the natural world. The parents' interest and involvement also validates, or adds value, to the child's efforts to learn about and care for the natural world.

Parents can benefit from involvement in a nature education program by increasing their own knowledge and appreciation of the natural world. They can also feel that their input is of value.

Approaches to Family Involvement

School-related activities. At school, parents might assist in planting flowers, participate in special nature celebrations (e.g., first day of spring), and join their children for the viewing of films or visits from naturalists. Parents might also be invited to participate in regularly-scheduled parent/child activities. These activities could include reading nature-related books together, doing nature art activities, and flying kites or cleaning up the school yard.

For parents who work outside the home during the day or who do not have a readily-accessible means of transportation, active participation in school activities is often difficult. You might invite these parents to become involved by assisting in the preparations for special activities and events. Perhaps there are phone calls they can make or props or snacks to prepare. A "Parent Work Night" might be organized, where parents who cannot come during the day, can still participate in what's happening at school.

While extra hands are always needed on field trips, parents need not be restricted to a chaperon position. Parents can also be invited to participate in the planning of the field trips. They may wish to host a visit to their own farms, gardens, or favorite picnic areas.

Providing information. Frequent written communication is another excellent way of keeping parents informed and involved. Teachers can share the joy and enthusiasm of a nature-related experience through a few sentences in their daily or weekly newsletter. They can share nature-related experiences through photos and experience stories on the display area at school.

Teachers can also make suggestions regarding related readings (for parents and/or children), family field trips (to nature centers, etc.) and at-home activities. While suggestions for parents may touch on recycling and other forms of conservation, it's important that family involvement ideas be offered as enjoyable suggestions not as urgent recommendations (Harlan, 1992).

Teachers can also provide information to families about the kinds of activities they can do at home and about the resources available in the community. Such resources may include nearby parks, zoos, and nature centers. Resources may also include books, videos, and special programs available through the public library or university. Be sure to involve parents in the development of a resource list.

Sharing interests, culture, and values. All parents should be given the opportunity and encouragement to share information and experiences about their own interests, culture, and values. They can be invited to share ethnic foods, customs, and special hobbies. They can be invited to tell stories and show pictures about their own experiences while growing up. They might also talk about trips to special places that they've visited.

Suggested Children's Books

Hines, Anna Grossnickle. *COME TO THE MEADOW*. Illustrations by author. Clarion, 1984. Fiction. Interest Level: Ages 3-6.

Long, Earlene. *GONE FISHING*. Illustrations by Richard Brown. Houghton, 1984. 32 pages. Fiction. Interest Level: Ages 2-5.

Stock, Catherine. *SOPHIE'S KNAPSACK*. Illustrations by author. Lothrop, 1988. Fiction. Interest Level: Ages 3-7.

Welber, Robert. *THE WINTER PICNIC*. Illustrations by Deborah Ray. Pantheon, 1970. Fiction. Interest Level: Ages 3-6.

Recommended Resource

Starting Small in the Wilderness: The Sierra Club Outdoors Guide for Families. M. Doan. San Francisco, CA: Sierra Club Books, 1979.

"Climb the mountains and get their good tidings. Nature's peace will flow into you as sunshine flows into trees. The winds will blow their own freshness into you, and the storms their energy, while cares will drop off like autumn leaves."

John Muir

Chapter 7
Enhancing Your Appreciation of Nature

Implementation Guideline #14: Enhance your own understanding and appreciation of the natural world.

While you need not be a scientist to help young children grow in understanding and appreciation of the natural world, you do need to model a personal interest in and respect for the world of nature. No matter where you presently stand in relation to nature appreciation, your personal continued growth in this area will add immensely to the quality of your program. There is certainly no one way to grow in understanding and appreciation of the natural world that will prove to be best for everyone. Each individual must find his or her own way of growing in knowledge and appreciation of the natural environment, and then give the time and energy needed to make it happen. Some people may turn to books; others to conferences, workshops, or naturalist-led nature walks. Still others may find that their best source of information and inspiration comes from nature itself and may choose to spend more time outdoors on their own—maybe through camping, hiking, bicycling, or taking frequent walks in the woods.

Educators should not overlook the many local, state, and regional environmental education associations and/or other groups focusing on the environment which might also be helpful. Following is a listing of some of these organizations, along with some selected books and environmental education training opportunities designed to help individuals enhance their personal appreciation of nature and increase their skills in leading environmental education activities with students of all ages.

Print Materials

The Earth Speaks.
S. Van Matre. and B. Weiler.
Warrenville, IL: The Institute for Earth Education, 1990.

Listening to Nature.
J. Cornell.
Nevada City, CA: Dawn Publications, 1987.

The Sense of Wonder.
Carson, R.
New York: Harper & Row, 1965.

Silent Spring.
Carson, R.
Boston: Houghton Mifflin, 1962.

Earth Education: A New Beginning.
Van Matre,
S. Warrenville, IL: The Institute for Earth Education, 1990.

Investigating Nature Through Outdoor Projects. Brown, V. Harrisburg, PA: Stackpole Books, 1983.

Environmental Organizations with Strong Environmental Education Components

Institute for Earth Education
P.O. Box 288,
Warrenville, IL 60555

National Audubon Society
950 Third Avenue,
New York, NY 10022

National Wildlife Federation
1412 16th St. NW
Washington, DC 20036

North American Association for Environmental Education
P.O. Box 400,
Troy, OH 45373

Sierra Club
1050 Mills Tower
San Francisco, CA 94104

Wilderness Society
729 Fifteenth St., NW,
Washington, DC 20005

Environmental Education Training Opportunities

In addition to conferences sponsored by professional environmental education organizations, the following training opportunities are also available.

Project WILD
P.O. Box 18060
Boulder, CO 80308-8060
Phone: (303) 444-2390
Project WILD training is often available at the state and local level, and is usually sponsored through the State Department of Education Inservice Training program.

NatureQuest Workshops
Sponsored by the National Wildlife Federation
1400 Sixteenth St., NW
Washington, DC 20036-2266
Phone: 1-800-245-5484 or (703) 790-4363
NatureQuest is designed as a training workshop for nature and science counselors, camp program directors, naturalists, and outdoor and environmental educators. Workshops are offered in locations across the country.

Education for Life Workshops
Education for Life Foundation,
14618 Tyler Foote Road,
Nevada City, CA 95959.
Phone (916)292-3775.
Developed by Joseph Cornell to help individuals deepen their own awareness of nature and learn how to help children grow in appreciation of the natural world.

Roger Tory Peterson Institute
110 Marvin Parkway
Jamestown, NY 14701
Phone (716)665-2473
Offers a variety of teacher training programs.

Part IV

Evaluating Your Program

"The cultivation of flowers and trees is the cultivation of the good, the beautiful, and the ennobling in man."
    J. Sterling Morton, Founder of Arbor Day

"If a child is to keep alive his inborn sense of wonder . . . he needs the companionship of at least one adult who can share it, rediscovering with him the joy, excitement and mystery of the world we live in."

Rachel Carson

Chapter 8
Fostering a Love of Nature Index

The purpose of this section is to provide you with a tool for evaluating and improving your own early childhood environmental education program. A "Fostering a Love of Nature Index" is provided which outlines the implementation guidelines presented in this book. Each of these guidelines is presented as a "Quality Indicator" against which you can compare practices within your own program. The Index also offers a format for evaluating your own strengths and needs in relation to each of the quality indicators and suggests the development of an Action Plan for enhancing your program in the areas where "needs" are identified.

Fostering A Love Of Nature Index

Quality Indicator #1

I introduce nature-related materials and activities in the different learning centers.

Implementation Score

Excellent	Good	Fair	Poor

Areas of Strength (Ways in which this is met):

Needs (Ways in which this could be improved):

Action Plan (Steps to further accomplish this goal):

Comments (Things to remember, concerns, questions, etc.):

Quality Indicator #2

I make animals and plants a
part of the classroom environment.

Implementation Score

Excellent	Good	Fair	Poor

Areas of Strength (Ways in which this is met):

Needs (Ways in which this could be improved):

Action Plan (Steps to further accomplish this goal):

Comments (Things to remember, concerns, questions, etc.):

Quality Indicator #3

I share pro-nature books with children.

Implementation Score

Excellent	Good	Fair	Poor

Areas of Strength (Ways in which this is met):

Needs (Ways in which this could be improved):

Action Plan (Steps to further accomplish this goal):

Comments (Things to remember, concerns, questions, etc.):

Quality Indicator #4

I encourage nature-related art activities.

Implementation Score

Excellent	Good	Fair	Poor

Areas of Strength (Ways in which this is met):

Needs (Ways in which this could be improved):

Action Plan (Steps to further accomplish this goal):

Comments (Things to remember, concerns, questions, etc.):

Quality Indicator #5

I introduce nature-related music and movement activities.

Implementation Score

Excellent	Good	Fair	Poor

Areas of Strength (Ways in which this is met):

Needs (Ways in which this could be improved):

Action Plan (Steps to further accomplish this goal):

Comments (Things to remember, concerns, questions, etc.):

Quality Indicator #6

I celebrate each of the seasons with special nature-related activities.

Implementation Score

Excellent	Good	Fair	Poor

Areas of Strength (Ways in which this is met):

Needs (Ways in which this could be improved):

Action Plan (Steps to further accomplish this goal):

Comments (Things to remember, concerns, questions, etc.):

Quality Indicator #7

I demonstrate the connection between the food we eat and the world of nature.

Implementation Score

Excellent	Good	Fair	Poor

Areas of Strength (Ways in which this is met):

Needs (Ways in which this could be improved):

Action Plan (Steps to further accomplish this goal):

Comments (Things to remember, concerns, questions, etc.):

Quality Indicator #8

I introduce a variety of nature-related themes and concepts through group activities.

Implementation Score

Excellent	Good	Fair	Poor

Areas of Strength (Ways in which this is met):

Needs (Ways in which this could be improved):

Action Plan (Steps to further accomplish this goal):

Comments (Things to remember, concerns, questions, etc.):

Quality Indicator #9

I display nature-related art and use materials from the natural world to decorate the classroom.

Implementation Score

Excellent	Good	Fair	Poor

Areas of Strength (Ways in which this is met):

Needs (Ways in which this could be improved):

Action Plan (Steps to further accomplish this goal):

Comments (Things to remember, concerns, questions, etc.):

Quality Indicator #10

I take the children on a variety of nature-study field trips.

Implementation Score

Excellent	Good	Fair	Poor

Areas of Strength (Ways in which this is met):

Needs (Ways in which this could be improved):

Action Plan (Steps to further accomplish this goal):

Comments (Things to remember, concerns, questions, etc.):

Quality Indicator #11

I introduce children to wildlife and other aspects of nature in and around the school yard.

Implementation Score

Excellent	Good	Fair	Poor

Areas of Strength (Ways in which this is met):

Needs (Ways in which this could be improved):

Action Plan (Steps to further accomplish this goal):

Comments (Things to remember, concerns, questions, etc.):

Quality Indicator #12

I individualize the program to meet special needs and interests.

Implementation Score

Excellent	Good	Fair	Poor

Areas of Strength (Ways in which this is met):

Needs (Ways in which this could be improved):

Action Plan (Steps to further accomplish this goal):

Comments (Things to remember, concerns, questions, etc.):

Quality Indicator #13

I invite parent participation in nature-related activities.

Implementation Score

Excellent	Good	Fair	Poor

Areas of Strength (Ways in which this is met):

Needs (Ways in which this could be improved):

Action Plan (Steps to further accomplish this goal):

Comments (Things to remember, concerns, questions, etc.):

Quality Indicator #14

I work to enhance my own understanding and appreciation of the natural world.

Implementation Score

Excellent	Good	Fair	Poor

Areas of Strength (Ways in which this is met):

Needs (Ways in which this could be improved):

Action Plan (Steps to further accomplish this goal):

Comments (Things to remember, concerns, questions, etc.):

Final Thoughts

Metamorphosis is a Greek word that means *to transform*. In the biological world, metamorphosis involves a complete change in appearance, character, and circumstances. It's a dramatic change that occurs on the way to maturity. Tadpoles emerge from eggs and then change into frogs. Larvae also hatch from eggs; they then enter a pupal stage and finally emerge as butterflies. The changes from one stage to another are dramatic indeed!

We usually think of metamorphosis as something that is unique to the life cycle of some of the lower animals. We look at ourselves as individuals and see that physically we have approximately the same form and structure as we had during infancy. We can also look at ourselves as a society of people. We've grown up with certain attitudes and behaviors and tend to carry these on to the next generation. We may thus conclude that metamorphosis is not a part of the human experience.

Yet a metamorphosis in the way we think and relate to the natural environment may be exactly what's needed to save the Earth. A close look at what's happening with the environment suggests that changes in the way we live must occur if we are to have a healthy planet. We can't continue relating to the Earth as if it were one huge garbage can or a bottomless well of resources. Changes in behavior, however, will not occur until there are changes in the way we think—and changes, to be effective for the future, must be embedded in the way we educate our children.

We must teach our children well, for they indeed are the future. While we now have guidelines for "best practices" in the **how** of early childhood education, still to be developed are guidelines on the **what**. The **how** is outlined in the "developmentally appropriate practices" developed and endorsed by the National Association for the Education of Young Children (Bredekamp, 1987). These guidelines are based on what is known about how young children learn, including their need for active involvement with concrete materials and interactions with people, their need for self-directed problem solving, and their need for gentle guidance and positive reinforcement.

The content (the **what**) of an early childhood curriculum is not as clearly defined. Tradition, social or cultural values, and parental desires usually provide some direction to what is included in the content, but these may vary considerably from one program to another. Some programs emphasize pre-academic skills and concepts; others emphasize social interaction. Few programs, however, operate on the premise that fostering a positive relationship with the natural environment is one of the most important things we can do for our children and the Earth.

Children are growing up in a society that values owning and controlling, where the natural world is viewed as an unlimited resource for humankind, and where many children have infrequent opportunities for positive interactions with the natural environment. A society that isolates children from nature does not teach understanding and appreciation of the natural environment, nor does it teach them that the Earth is a community to which they belong.

Early childhood educators have an important role to play in bringing about a societal metamorphosis. We, as a society, have lived inside a cocoon-like structure for too long—a structure which keeps us from seeing and experiencing a larger world. It's time to emerge from this cocoon and move into a new way of relating to Planet Earth—and the place to start is with the children.

References

Bredekamp, S. (Ed.). (1987). *Developmentally Appropriate Practice in Early Childhood Programs Serving Children from Birth Through Age 8: Expanded Edition*. Washington, DC: National Association for the Education of Young Children.

Burrus-Bammel, L., & Bammel, G. (1990). Outdoor/environmental education—An overview for the wise use of Leisure. *JOPERD, 61* (4), 49-22.

Caduto, M. (1983). A review of environmental values education. *Journal of Environmental Education, 14* (3), 13-20.

Caduto, M.J. & Bruchac, J. (1991). *Keepers of the Animals: Teacher's Guide*. Golden, CO: Fulcrum Publishing.

Carson, R. (1956). *The Sense of Wonder*. New York: Harper & Row.

Cohen, M. (1984). Prejudice against Nature. Freeport, ME: Cobblesmith.

Cohen, S. (1992). Promoting ecological awareness in children. *Childhood Education, 60* (5), 258-260.

Cornell, J. (1989). *Sharing the Joy of Nature*. Nevada City, CA: Dawn Publications.

Cornell, J.B. (1979). *Sharing Nature With Children*. Nevada City, CA: Ananda Publications.

Crompton, J.L. & Sellar, C. (1981). Do outdoor education experiences contribute to positive development in the affective domain? *Journal of Environmental Education, 12* (4), 21-29.

Disinger, J.F. (1985/86). Current trends in environmental education. *Journal of Environmental Education, 17* (2), 1-3.

Earth Works Group. (1989) *50 Simple Things You Can Do to Save the Earth*. Berkeley, CA: Earthworks Press.

Elkind, D. (1988). *Miseducation: Preschoolers at risk*. New York: Alfred A. Knopf.

Harlan, J.D. (1992). *Science Experiences for the Early Childhood Years*. New York: Macmillan Publishing Company.

Henderson, K.A. (1990). Deep ecology and outdoor recreation—Incompatible? *JOPERD, 61* (3), 77-80.

Katz, L. (1987). What should young children be learning? *ERIC Digest*, Urbana Illinois: Clearninghouse on Elementary and Early Childhood Education.

References

Kramer, D.C. ((1989). Animals in the Classroom. Menlo Park, CA: Addison-Wesley Publishing Company.

Miles, J.C. (1986-87). Wilderness as a learning place. *Journal of Environmental Education, 18* (2), 33-40.

More, T. A. (1977). An analysis of wildlife in children's stories. *Children, nature, and the environment: Proceedings of a symposium fair.* USDA Forest Service General Technical Report NE. 30.

Priest, S. (1986). Redefining outdoor education: A matter of many relationships. *Journal of Environmental Education, 17* (3), 13-15.

Ramsey, J.M.; Hungerford, H.R.; & Volk, T.L. (1992). Environmental education in the K-12 curriculum: Finding a niche. *Journal of Environmental Education, 23* (2), 35-45.

Schicker, L. (1988). Planning for children and wildlife begins at home. *Journal of Environmental Education, 19* (4), 13-21.

Spodek, B, Saracho, O.N., & Davis, M.D. (1987). *Foundations of Early Childhood Education.* Englewood Cliffs, NJ: Prentice-Hall, Inc.

Trant, A. (1986). An introduction to environmental education in the European community. *Journal of Outdoor Education, 20,* 16-29.

Van Matre, S. (1972). *Acclimatization.* Martinsville, IN: American Camping Association, Inc.

Van Matre, S. (1990). *Earth Education: A New Beginning.* Warrenville, IL: The Institute for Earth Education.

Widerstrom, A.H. (1986). Educating young handicapped children: What can early childhood education contribute? *Childhood Education, 63* (2), 78-83.

Index

A

acclimatization 17
adventure playground 132
aesthetic development 7, 47
Animal Prints 53
animal tracks 53, 105, 127, 128, 130
Animals in the Classroom 31
   guidelines for selecting 31
   introducing to the children 145
Ants' Eye View 134
Apple activities 67
aquarium 30, 32, 35, 121
Aquatic Snails 34
Art Center 30
Artistic Arrangements 57

B

beauty hunt 48
Big Bad Wolf Syndrome 39
Big Book 42, 45, 89, 118
Biological Supply Companies 183
Block Center 28, 30
butterfly meadow 133

C

camouflage 106
carrot plant 89
Charades 66
child-centered approach 9
Children's Global Flag 111
Coconut 99
collage 15, 48, 49, 67, 114
Community resources 121
Compost 67, 136
Crayfish 33

D

developmentally appropriate practices 9, 101, 173
Disabilities 146
Discovery Center 28
Dramatic Play Center 30

E

Earth Flag 111
earthworm 14, 32, 127
ecosystemic 18, 19
ekistic 18, 19
enjoyment factor 16
Environmental education goals 5, 10, 11
ethics 19
Experience Stories 118, 119

F

Fall 30, 67, 69, 84, 85
Fears 14, 143
field notes 122, 123
field trips 14, 20, 23, 113-121
Finger Plays 44
Flour 94
food 23, 87
Food Plants 88

G

games 134
garden 14, 137
gardening 137
gardening tools 30
Goals and Objectives 10
group activities 23, 101-107

177

H

Halloween 68
Harvest 69
Hide and Seek 134
Hiding Game 106

I

Icicle 72
immersion 17
implementation guidelines 23
Infants and Toddlers 147
Infusion approach 23
Interpersonal 18, 19
intrapersonal relationships 18, 19
intuition 5, 17

J

journal 118, 119, 123

K

"key characteristics" 9
kinship 19

L

Language Experience Center 27, 30
Leading the Blind 135
Leaf activities 67
learning centers 23-30, 27, 30
Lily Pad Jump 135
listening place 138

M

Manipulative Center 27, 30
Math Center 28, 30
meadows 20, 127
metamorphosis 173, 174
Mobiles 54
Mother's Day 47, 51
movement 23, 62, 162
multicultural 22
Multicultural Books 42, 43
multicultural experiences 13, 22
multimodal 17, 101
multimodal learning 13, 17, 18
music 10, 23, 61, 62
Music and Movement 59
Music Center 28, 30
Musical Instruments 64
Mystery Eater 135

N

Native American 42, 65
Natural Straws 83
nature area 131, 133
Nature Boxes 58
nature center 15
Nature Songs 63
nature walk 9, 14

O

Onion bulb 92

P

parent participation 23, 149-150
Peanut Butter 95
Photos 55
pineapple plant 89
Plants in the Classroom 36
Playground Alternatives 131
Poetry 44
Popcorn 98
prejudice against nature 40
pro-nature books 23, 39-45, 185-187
Pumpkin activities 67, 96

Q

quiet retreat 114

R

recycling 11, 21, 37
relationships 18
Rice 97
Rubbings 50

S

Science Center 28, 30
Science Education 3, 5, 6
sense of connectedness 4, 7
sensorimotor 6, 10
Sharing Circle 103, 104, 115, 117
snow 14, 30, 73, 75, 116, 191
social development 18
sound-catchers 116
special needs 23, 143, 146
stewardship 4
Still-hunting 114
sweet potato vine 88

T

teachable moments 9
Terrarium 30, 36, 109, 110
Texture Table 14, 28, 30
The Mystery Eater 135
Treasure Hunt 134
tree houses 131

V

values education 19
videos 45, 65
visualization 117

W

wildflowers 15, 21, 48, 115
Wildlife Hunt 122
Wildlife in the City 121
Wildlife in the Country 126
Window Hangings 51
worm bin 136

Appendices

Appendix A
Biological Supply Companies

Carolina Biological Supply Company, 2700 York Road, Burlington, NC 27215

Connecticut Valley Biological Supply Company, 82 Valley Road, P.O. Box 326, Southhampton, MA 01073

Fisher Scientific/Educational Materials Division, 4901, W. LeMoyne Street, Chicago, IL 60651

Kons Scientific Company, P.O. Box 3, Germantown, WI 53022-0003

Nasco, 901 Janesville Avenue, Fort Atkinson, WI 53538

Ward's Natural Science Establishment, 5100 West Henrietta Road, P.O. Box 92912, Rochester, NY 14692-9012

Appendix B
Pro-Nature Children's Books

A Dog's Book of Birds by Peter Parnall. The ever-present dog in this story seeks out, chases, and sometimes hides in this playful picture-book guide to a variety of feathered folk.

Alfalfa Hill by Peter Parnall. Winter was coming to Alfalfa Hill. The animals raced with nature throughout the fall, scurrying to prepare for the cold and hungry time ahead. And then it came— quietly, soft and white, the snow transformed the land into the strange new world of winter.

Anybody Home? Aileen Fisher. A young child finds and wonders about the homes of different animals. How she wishes she could see inside!

A Summer Day by Douglas Florian. A family takes a trip to the country and enjoys a summer day of relaxation and fun.

Beaver at Long Pond by William George. As the other animals at Long Pond settle down for the night, Beaver leaves his lodge, begins searching for food, and starts his nightly adventure.

Be Nice to Spiders by Margaret Bloy Graham. When Billy moved into an apartment, he left his pet spider, Helen, at the Zoo. Soon after, the animals at the zoo all became happy and contented—all because Helen was spinning webs and catching flies. One day, in preparation for the Mayor's visit, all the webs were swept away and Helen felt a need to go into hiding. Soon the flies were back again and the animals were miserable once more. Helen solved the problem once more and won a permanent place of honor for herself in the zoo.

Chickens Aren't the Only Ones by Ruth Heller. Interesting text and beautiful illustrations tell a story about animals that lay eggs.

Coyote Cry by Byrd Baylor. A story about the gradual change in a young boy's attitudes toward the coyote. Grandfather's words alone, were not enough to convince Antonio to think of the coyote in any other way than that of enemy. A series of events, however, help Antonio understand the meaning of the coyote's song that is sung to the moon.

Everybody Needs a Rock by Byrd Baylor. More to be treasured than bicycles, goldfish, and horses is having just the right rock. Finding such a rock, however, requires a great deal of thought and care. Presented in poetic form are ten suggestions on how to find the rock that is just right for you.

Fishes by Brain Wildsmith. Paintings in shimmering blues and greens and purples depict assemblies of fishes, according to their kind.

Georgia Music by Helen Griffith. An old man and his granddaughter listened to the summer sounds of Georgia as they went about their work—sounds like the cricket chirps, the tree frog trills and the noisy songs of a sassy mockingbird. Eventually, the time came for the old man to leave his Georgia cabin. The girl was troubled to see her grandfather become sad and quiet in his new home. One day, she found a way of bringing back the Georgia music and making her grandfather laugh again.

Guess Who My Favorite Person Is by Byrd Baylor. A charming story about two friends engaged in the game of naming their favorite things—from favorite ladybugs in the alfalfa field to the favorite time of the day. Many "favorites" are tied to the beauty and wonder of the natural world.

Hawk, I'm your Brother by Byrd Baylor. Rudy Soto wants more than anything to fly. People tell him that he will never fly, but Rudy is not convinced. He steals a baby hawk from its nest, thinking that somehow it will help him fly. Rudy learns that he can almost fly, when he finally lets the hawk go free.

High in the Mountains by Ruth Yaffe Radin. A young child describes a day spent near Grandpa's house in the mountains honor for herself in the zoo.

I'm in Charge of Celebrations by Byrd Baylor. A delightful story about a young girl and her private celebrations. It's not the calendar that proclaims a day of celebration, but events and experiences in the out-of-doors—experiences like watching a triple rainbow with a jackrabbit, seeing a green cloud take the shape of a parrot, and making eye-to-eye contact with a coyote on a rocky trail. Poetic text and extraordinary illustrations combine to bring to life the wonders of the Southwest desert.

Inch by Inch by Leo Lionni. A story about a clever and charming inchworm who measures his way to freedom. He measures the robin's tail, the flamingo's neck, the heron's legs, and a whole hummingbird. He faces his greatest challenge, however, when asked to measure the nightingale's song.

Let's Be Nature's Friend by Jack Stokes. Through lively verse and colorful pictures, Jack Stokes offers suggestions on how to take care of the earth.

Milkweed Days by Jane Yolen. Milkweed days are the long, lazy days of late-summer. They are the days when three children like to play in the sunny, fragrant meadow behind the old barn. There they discover the secrets of the milkweed.

Night in the Country by Cynthia Rylant. A story about the sounds and wonders of a night in the country.

Say It! by Charlotte Zolotow. A girl and her mother take a walk on a golden, windy autumn day. They experience a special time together as they delight in the beauty of the season and each other.

Signs Along the River by Kayo Robertson. Information on how to read the natural landscape. Nature doesn't often shout its story; the landscape reveals itself to us silently and with subtlety.

Sometimes I Dance Mountains by Byrd Baylor. In text and illustrations, a young dancer dances mountains and whirlwinds, bubbles and bugs, water, stars and wind—and in doing so, realizes that dancing offers a way of becoming some other thing, some other feeling, some other place and time.

Summer Is . . . by Charlotte Zolotow. A walk through the seasons with a sharing of the joys experienced throughout the year.

The Lace Snail by Betsy Byars. The gift of the snail is the making and sharing of lace. When questioned about this special ability, the snail's simple response reflects a depth of understanding about the nature of life.

The Mixed-Up Chameleon by Eric Carle. A bored chameleon wishes it could be more like all the other animals it sees, but soon decides it would rather just be itself. This delightfully illustrated and formatted book is both fun and instructive. Children learn something about the ways of a chameleon, but, in the process, learn about self acceptance, as well.

The Quiet Evening by Thacher Hurd. A story about the coming of evening—a time when everything is quiet. The ocean has wrapped its arms around all its fish, and the earth is turning silently in the starry night.

The Snail's Spell by Joanne Ryder. A poem of change inviting the reader to live for a short time like a different creature, in an ever-changing garden world.

The Snowy Day by Ezra Jack Keats. A young boy's experience with snow—from enjoyment in the out-of-doors on a wintry day to the fear of the snow disappearing during the night. think of the coyote in any other way than that of enemy. A series of events, however, help Antonio understand the meaning of the coyote's song that is sung to the moon.

Where The Forest Meets the Sky by Jeannie Baker. This is a story about a walk with a young boy and his father among the ancient trees of a tropical rain forest. Extraordinary lifelike collage illustrations enhance the text.

William and Boomer by Lindsay Barrett George. Young William longs to swim like Boomer, his new pet goose. As the summer passes he learns to do just that.

Appendix C
Themes and Books

Animals
A Bird Can Fly, Douglas Florian
Animal Homes, Brian Wildsmith
Animals, Animals, Eric Carle
How Animals Sleep, Millicent Selsam
Large as Life Animals, Joanna Cole
The Petting Zoo, Jack Hanna
What Animals Do, Richard Scarry
Wild Animal Families, Margaret Davidson
Wild Animals, Tony Chen

Birds
Amazing Birds, Alexandra Parsons
It's Nesting Time, Roma Gans
Tony's Birds, M.E. Selsam

Bugs
Backyard Bugs, JoAnne Nelson
Bugs, Bugs, Bugs, Better Homes & Gardens

Butterflies
From Egg to Butterfly, Marlene Reidel
I Like Butterflies, by Gladys Conklin
Remember the Butterflies, Anna Grossnickle Hines
Where Does the Butterfly Go When It Rains?, May Garelick

Caterpillars
I Like Caterpillars, by Gladys Conklin
Terry and the Caterpillars, Millicent E. Selsam
The Very Hungry Caterpillar, Eric Carle

Chameleons
Chameleons: Dragons in the Trees, James Martin
The Mixed-Up Chameleon, Eric Carle

Crayfish
A House for Hermit Crab, Eric Carle

Crickets
If I Were a Cricket, Kazue Mizumura
The Very Quiet Cricket, Eric Carle

Endangered Animals
Danger on the African Grassland, Elisabeth Sackett

Fall
Autumn Harvest, Alvin Tresselt
Autumn Story, Jill Barklem
Autumn, Lucille Wood
Fall, Ron Hirschi

Fish
A Salmon for Simon, Betty Waterton
Fish, Steve Parker

Flowers
Hope for the Flowers, Trina Paulus
The Flowers, Marion Mineau.

Forests and Woods
A Day in the Woods, Ronald M. Fisher
Children of the Forest, a picture book by Elsa Beskow
See Through the Forest, Millicent E. Selsam
Two Tiny Mice, Alan Baker
When the Woods Hum, Joanne Ryder
Wonders of the Forest, Francene Sabin

Frogs
Amazing Frogs and Toads, Barry Clarke
One Green Frog, Yvonne Hooker

Gardens
Let's Grow A Garden, Gyo Fujikawa
Vegetable Garden, Douglas Florian
Who Goes There in My Garden?, Carol Cornelius
Willie's Garden, Myra McGee

Ladybugs
Ladybug, Ladybug, Fly Away Home, J. Hawes
The Grouchy Ladybug, Eric Carle

Leaves
A First Look at Leaves, Millicent E. Selsam and Joyce Hunt
Red Leaf, Yellow Leaf, Lois Ehlert

Moths
The Apple and the Moth, Iela Mari and Enzo Mari

Mountains
Up, Up the Mountain, Aileen Fisher

Night
Animals At Night, Sharon Peters
Night is Coming, W. Nikola-Lisa

Owls
I Am an Owl, Yvonne Hooker
Owl Moon, Jane Yolen
The Owl and the Woodpecker, Brian Wildsmith

Plants
Milkweed Days, Jane Yolen
The Plant Sitter, Gene Zion and Margaret Graham

Ponds and Lakes
Fishing at Long Pond, William T. George
Loon Lake, Ron Hirschi
Pond Life: Watching Animals Find Food, Herbert Wong & Matthew Vessel

Rocks
The Rock, Peter Parnall

Seasons
Around the Year, Elsa Beskow
My Five Seasons, Aliki
Seasons, Brian Wildsmith
Seasons?, S. Leslie

Seeds
From Seed to Plant, Gail Gibbons
Seeds and More Seeds, Millicent E. Selsam
The Carrot Seed, Ruth Krauss
The Tiny Seed, Eric Carle

Snakes
Amazing Snakes, Alexandra Parsons

Snow
The Snowy Day, Ezra Jack Keats
White Snow, Bright Snow, Ezra Jack Keats

Spiders
Amazing Spiders, Alexandra Parsons
Be Nice to Spiders, Margaret Bloy Graham
The Spider Makes A Web, Joan Lexau
The Very Busy Spider, Eric Carle

Spring
Children of the Forest, a picture book by Elsa Beskow.
My Spring Robin, Anne Rockwell
The Story of the Root Children, Sybylle von Olfers

Squirrels
Busy, Busy Squirrels, Colleen Stanley
Squirrels, Brian Wildsmith

Summer
Summer Is, C. Zolotow

Trees
A Tree is Nice, Janice May Udry
Have You Seen Trees?, Joanne Oppenheim
Once There Was a Tree, Natalie Romanova
Our Tree, Herbert Wong and Matthew Vessel
The Giving Tree, Shel Silverstein
The Lorax, Theodor Geisel (Dr. Seuss)
Trees, Usborne First Nature Book

Whales
I Wonder If I'll See a Whale, Frances Ward Weller
The Whales' Song, Dyan Sheldon
Whales, Gail Gibbons
Winter Whale, Joanne Ryder

Wind
Gilbert and the Wind, Marie Hall Ets

Winter
Plants in Winter, Joanna Cole

Appendix D
Resources for Teachers

ANNOTATED BIBLIOGRAPHY*
developed by
Melinda Geithmann, M.Ed.

Acclimatization. S. Van Matre. Martinsville, IN: American Camping Association, 1989.

This activity book focuses on outdoor education and immersion in nature projects. Each day of the nature program focuses on a different natural environment. The goal of the program is to break down the barriers between persons and nature and for a person to be surrounded by and involved with the environment.

Adventures with a Hand Lens. R. Headstrom. New York: Dover Publications, 1976.

An activity book which features the use of a magnifying lens to examine plants and animals. The book is divided into 50 activities.

Airy Canary Learns to Fly. Commonwealth of Virginia: Department of Air Pollution Control.

A coloring book which tells the story of a canary who is trying to fly, but air pollution is affecting him.

---

* Materials available for loan through:
   Center for Environmental Programs
   Bowling Green State University
   Bowling Green, Ohio 43403
   Phone 419/372-8207

An Early Start to Nature. R. Richards. New York: Simon & Schuster, 1989.

Provides information and activities concerning trees, plants, birds, invertebrates, water life, and the moon and stars. Emphasis is placed on the child's practical investigation at first hand.

An Early Start to Science. R. Richards, M. Collis, D. Kincaid. New York: Simon &Schuster, 1989.

Provides information and activities concerning gardens, people, color, collecting, waterplay and homeplay. The emphasis is on practical investigation at first hand.

An Environmental Education Guide for Teachers. P. Gail. Cleveland, OH: Institute for Environmental Education, 1974.

A publication addressed to teachers, and organized as suggestions on how they might integrate environmental/community studies into their present courses. Included are opinions about training, resources, grading, evaluation, and the involvement of colleagues, administrators, and community persons. Chapters focus on incorporating environmental problem studies into teaching, planning the investigation and preparing the study, evaluating/grading environmental studies, finding and using resources, and building a support base in the school and community.

Animals in the Classroom. D. Kramer. New York: Addison Wesley, 1989.

Sourcebook for teachers interested in keeping a variety of small animals in the classroom- earthworms, snails, crickets, hermit crabs, frogs, hamsters, birds- 28 animals covered in all. For each, this book explains natural history, how to obtain, housing and diet, observations and activities, and what to do when the project is over.

Avoiding Infusion Confusion: A Practical Handbook for Infusing Environmental Activities into your Classroom. H. Hayden, M. Oltman, R. Thompson-Tucker, S. Wood. Amherst Junction, WI: Central Wisconsin Environmental Station, 1987.

This handbook combines activities contained in selected widely used environmental education programs with five content areas: Art, Health, Language Arts, Sciences and Social Studies. These resources are organized according to the content area they relate to.

Beastly Neighbors. M. Rights. Boston, MA: Little, Brown & Co, 1981.

This activity book focuses on animals and plants in urban environments. Information and activities focusing on trees, birds, air, insects, rodents and recycling. Grades Pre K-12.

Beautiful Junk: Creative Classroom Uses for Recyclable Materials. K. Brackett & R. Manley. Carthage IL: Fearon Teacher Aids, 1990.

This activity book explains over 200 creative ways to recycle boxes, cans, flyers, and other throwaways into classroom equipment and materials for student projects. The projects are illustrated, and many diagrams and patterns are provided. Describes sources of free and inexpensive materials and includes an index of activities.

Beyond the Classroom: Exploration of Schoolground and Backyard. C. Roth, C. Cervoni, T. Wellnitz, & E. Arms. Lincoln, MA: Massachusetts Audubon Society, 1988.

Provides 30 activities in earth science, life science and physical science. Each activity is described by grade level, duration, group size, skills, materials/site needs, focus and procedure.

Bridging Early Childhood and Nature Education. Jamestown, NY: Roger Tory Peterson Institute, 1991.

Report begins with an overview of Roger Peterson's recollections of childhood experiences which influenced his development as a naturalist, and affirms the value of nature education for young children, offers basic reference questions, a discussion of developmental appropriateness and guidelines for selecting activities for young children.

Bubbles, Rainbows, and Worms: Science Experiments for Preschool Children. S. Brown. Mt. Rainier, MD: Gryphon House, Inc., 1981.

An activity book for preschool children and their teachers which focuses on science experiments with air, animals, the environment, plants, the senses, and water.

The Bug Book. H. Danks. New York: Workman Publishing, 1987.

This field guide to insects offers full illustrations and descriptions for 24 common insects. It also gives tips on catching bugs, instructions for keeping them safely at home, and suggestions for Bug Bottle Projects. Includes plastic "Bug Bottle" with perforated lid.

Bugs Don't Bug Us. (video) Eureka, MT: Bo Peep Productions, 1991.

This video introduces many of the most common insects, and children in the tape interact comfortably with them. Ages 2-7. Video length: 35 minutes.

Bugs to Bunnies: Hands-on Animal Science Activities for Young Children. K. Goin, E. Ripp, K. Nastasi-Solomon. New York: Chatterbox Press, 1989.

Features many hands-on activities to teach young children the science of animals. Units include insects, spiders, amphibians, reptiles, fish, birds and mammals and discusses the physical characteristics, diet, defenses, habitats and reproduction of these animals. Each unit features stories, activity ideas for large and small groups, and reproducible science sheets.

California State Environmental Education Guide, The. C. Sly, L. Comnes, C. Cuomo. Hayward, CA: Alameda County Office of Education, 1988.

Provides teachers and other educators with classroom lessons and instructional techniques that build a fundamental understanding of the environment. The guide is aimed at grades kindergarten through sixth and consists of eight instructional units and six action projects. Kindergarten instructional units are concerned with "the diversity of life'" and "caring for the environment."

Catalog of Elementary Environmental Education Recources. White Bear Lake, MN: Minnesota Curriculum Services Center.

Catalog is divided into two major categories: curriculum materials and non-curricular items such as booklets, brochures, directories and audio-visual materials. Curricular subjects include acid rain, agriculture, animals, aquatic conservation energy, natural history, plants, recycling and urban environments.

Childhood Education: (1992) Vol. 68, Number 5 S. Cohen, (Ed.) Wheaton, MD: Journal Of The Association For Childhood Education International.

Highlights many articles on children (infancy through adolescence) and the environment. Also contains an article about resources for environmental education by Dr. Ruth A. Wilson Ph.D. of Bowling Green State University.

City Safaris. C. Shaffer & E. Fielder. San Francisco, CA: Sierra Club Books, 1987.

Shows teachers and group leaders how to plan field trips in cities. Children can explore vacant lots, discover the way the city obtains its food, goods and services, trace a city's history and envision its future. The activities, both structured and unstructured, can be adapted for use with a single child to a large group, and range from half hour walks to a month long project. Grades Pre K-12.

Creating Environmental Publications. J. Zehr, M. Gross, R. Zimmerman. Stevens Point, WI: UW— SP Foundation Press, Inc:

This resource guide is intended for individuals who wish to publish their own environmental booklets, posters, and newsletters.

Creative Environmental Education Activities for Children. Environmental Education Curriculum Guide. Tennessee Valley Authority (Land Between the Lakes). Golden Pond, KY: TVA, 1984.

Twenty-seven activities have been compiled to assist teachers in incorporating environmental methods and techniques into their preschool curricula. Each activity includes: activity number, time required to complete the activity, subject area(mathematics, science, language arts, art, music), title, objectives, list of materials needed, references and procedures.

Discover The World: Empowering Children to Value Themselves, Others and the Earth. S.Hopkins & J. Winters, Philadelphia, PA: New Society Publishers, 1990.

This is a handbook for teachers, parents and other caregivers seeking to create an environment in which children aged 3-12 can build self-esteem while becoming respectfully aware of others. It is full of easily applicable ideas and resources. Activity charts are organized to encourage understanding and appreciation of diversity and respect for the earth through art, science, large and fine motor skills, and language.

E is for Environment. P.K. Sinclair, New Providence, NJ; R.R.Bowker, 1992.

This book is an annotated bibliography of children's books with environmental themes.

Early Childhood and Science. M. McIntyre. Washington, DC: National Science Teacher's Association, 1984.

A collection of articles reprinted from *Science and Children* magazine. Chapters include "What is science for young children?," "Approaches to science teaching," "Seasonal science activities," "Using science content areas," and " Curriculum needs and complements." Activities are included.

Earth Book for Kids. L. Schwartz. Santa Barbara, CA: The Learning Works, Inc., 1990.
Offers children and their families a variety of ways to learn about the environment. Factual information and activities focus on recycling, air, land and water, plant and animal habitats, and Earth Day.

Earth Child. K. Sheehan & M. Waidner. Tulsa, OK: Council Oak Books, 1991.
This activity book includes exercises, games, stories, and songs to be shared by children and adults. It also includes many ecology-related resources for adults, and annotated lists of children's nature books. Topics cover the role of the sun, earth celebrations, habitats, compassion for animals, endangered species, and peacekeeping practices. Goals of the activities include nurturing imagination, empathy, and a deeper understanding of the earth, and teaching conservation and the interconnectedness of all living things.

Earthkeepers. S. Van Matre & B. Johnson. Warrenville, IL: Institute for Earth Education, 1988.
An environmental program for 10-12 year olds which helps them) understand how energy and materials tie all life together; experience positive feelings when they are in touch with nature; increase their understanding of, feelings for, and harmony with the earth and its life.

Earthways. C. Petrash. Mt. Rainier, Maryland: Gryphon House, 1992.
Earthways is filled with hands-on nature crafts and seasonal activities to enhance environmental awareness. The activities are carefully written and beautiful illustrated. Children play with the elements of earth, air and water. Children learn firsthand about their dependence on the earth. They can learn how to take stalks of wheat and turn them into flour for making bread, how to be a creator and not just a consumer by making gifts, how to make butter and grow food (even in the city), and how to make outdoor playhouses.

Earthy Tunes. (audiocassette) M. Miche´. Berkeley, CA: Song Trek Music.
Seventeen songs about animals, birds, insects and plants are featured on this tape. Lyrics included. Ages 3-11 years.

Ecolokids Activity Book. K. McDonnel. Lubbock, TX: Capaz Enterprises, 1990.
Provides ten activities for primary age children which focus on conservation.

Environmental Education in the Urban Setting: Rationale and Teaching Activities. H. Coon & M. L. Bowman. Columbus, OH: ERIC Clearinghouse for Science, Mathematics, and Environmental Education, 1976.
Discusses a point of view about the opportunities for environmental education in urban schools and gives ideas and activities designed for student use in grades K-12. The activiites fall into five subject areas: science, mathematics, social studies, language arts and fine arts.

Essential Learnings in Environmental Education. D. Hanselman, M. Raghunathan, K. Sarabiihai (editors). Troy, OH: North American Association for Environmental Education, 1990.
Provides building blocks for designing and reviewing environmental education programs and activities. The book contains basic concepts that are necessary to form a solid understanding of the environment, and breaks them down into their component concepts and identifying level at which these can concepts can be taught.

Eye-openers! How to Choose and Use Children's Books about Real People, Places and Things. B. Kobrin. New York: Penguin Books, 1988.
The author reviews more than 500 nonfiction books which can encourage children to read and can be linked to children's everyday experiences. Books about animals and without words are discussed.

Evergreen, Everblue. (audiocassette) Raffi. Universal City, CA: MCA Records, 1990.
Eleven songs sung by Raffi which focus on ecology and environmental awareness.

Explore and Experiment. J. Perez. Bridgeport CT: First Teacher Press, 1988.

Provides science and nature experiments for preschool children. Topics include air, water, plants, animals, the earth and crafts from recyclables.

Exploring Our Environment: Plants. (Resource Guide and Student Materials 1&2) S. DeRoo. Novato, CA: Ann Arbor Publishers,1977.

A resource/curriculum guide emphasizing exploring and discovering the natural world. The science program for the very early years is taught by the season and the availability of materials. The curriculum guide is designed for grades K-6 and includes primary and secondary student materials booklets.

Exploring Science in Early Childhood: A Developmental Approach. K. Lind. Albany, NY: Delmar Publishers Inc., 1991.

Presents an organized sequential approach to creating a developmentally appropriate science curriculum for preschool and primary age children. An emphasis is placed on three types of learning: naturalistic, informal, and structured. Students investigate life, physical, and earth science as well as health and nutrition.

Friends of the Flowers. (video) J. Davis. Toledo, OH: Joyce Davis 'n Puppets, 1992.

This video presents information about insects and flowers, how to make and use puppets for nature instruction, directions for nature crafts and snacks, and activities which relate to flowers and insects. Video length: 30 minutes.

For Kids Who Love Animals. L. Koebneer. Living Planet Press: Venice, CA, 1991.

A book written for children which provides facts about animals and their habitats, describes how some animals are mistreated or exploited, and ways for children to help endangered species.

Fostering A Sense Of Wonder During The Early Childhood Years. R. Wilson. Greyden Press: Columbus, OH, 1993.

A curriculum guide designed to infuse Environmental Education into all aspects of an Early Childhood program.

The Frog Chorus: Songs, Stories, and Activities. (audiocassette) D. Stokes. Milwaukee, WI: Schlitz Audobon Center, 1991.

This audiocassette includes 22 songs about nature: some songs include stories and instructions for the use of puppets in activities. Lyrics are also included.

Good Earth Art: Environmental Art for Kids. M. Kohl & C. Gainer. Bellingham, WA: Bright Ring Publishing, 1991.

Over 200 activities use recycled and natural materials, and teach environmental responsibility. Each activity is coded for type of material, age range, group or individual project and special safety concerns. Collages, weaving, printmaking, wood-scrap sculpture and painting activities are routes to understanding both science and nature.

Good Planets are Hard to Find! R. Dehr and R. Bazar. Vancouver, BC, Canada: Earth Beat Press, 1990.

A resource book for children organized in a dictionary format. Topics include energy conservation, animal habitats, and protecting wildlife.

Grow Lab: A Complete Guide to Gardening in the Classroom. E. Pranis, J. Hale. : Burlington, VT: National Gardening Association, 1991.

A horticultural resource for use with an indoor classroom garden. The guide gives step-by-step planting instructions to tips on seed varieties, from instructions for leaving the garden over vacation to plans for a build it yourself model, from hints on building support for the program to innovative ideas for integrating gardening activities into the curriculum.

Grow Your Own Tree- Teacher's Kit. M. Steinheider. Nebraska City, NE: The National Arbor Day Foundation, 1990.

This curriulum, designed for lower elementary grades, teaches the value of trees and pride in environmental stewardship. The instructional package includes: 2 posters for classroom display, planting materials for 25 individuals, an Arbor Day booklet, two filmstrips, 2 audiocassettes which accompany the filmstrips, and a teacher's guide.

Growing Ideas; A Journal of Garden-Based Learning. Burlington, VT: National Gardening Association, 1992.

Growing Ideas is just one of a range of Grow Lab Indoor Gardening program resources to help use plants in the classroom. The" Growing Ideas" Newsletter provides useful classroom-tested activities, horticultural tips, funding ideas, and resources for using plants to enrich classroom learning.

A Guide to Curriculum Planning in Environmental Education. Madison, WI: Wisconsin Department of Public Instruction, 1991.

Publication designed to be used as an aid in planning and implementing a school district environmental education curriculum. The guide emphasizes the infusion of environmental topics into all curricular areas.

"The Having of Wonderful Ideas" and Other Essays on Teaching and Learning. E. Duckworth. New York, NY: Teachers College Press, 1987.

Eleanor Duckworth brings together her wide-ranging writings on Piaget and teaching, many published here for the first time. While touching on many subjects- from science, math, and language, to thinking, teaching, learning, evaluation, and teacher education- each of these essays supports the author's deeply felt belief that "the having of wonderful ideas is the essence of intellectual development," and that the focus of teacher education should be on the learner's point of view. Her constant concern is to encourage an approach to education that allows "occasions" for learners, whether children or teachers, to construct their own knowledge.

Hands-on Nature: Information and Activities for Exploring the Environment with Children. J.Lingelbach (editor). Woodstock, VT: Vermont Institute of Natural Science, 1986.

Nature "workshops" are grouped into four separate chapters: Adaptations, Habitats, Cycles, and Designs of Nature. Within the chapters, the workshops are arranged in seasonal order. Within each workshop there are two main parts: an informational essay, which includes resources, and an activity section. Grades K-6.

Home for Pearl, A. (video) Washington, DC: U.S. Fish and Wildlife Service, 1990.

Teaches children about wildlife habitat and heightens their awareness of what wildlife needs to survive. The video consists of four parts: The Robin, Habitat Diversity, Predators, and The Right Home for Pearl. Video length: 70 minutes. Grades K-6.

Home for Pearl, A. E. Lambeth & M. Westervelt. Washington, DC: U.S. Fish and Wildlife Service, 1990.

Instructional guide which accompanies the video of the same name. Like the video, the guide is divided into four parts. Included in each section is an overview, student objectives, a story summary, key words, discussion questions, ideas for follow-up activiites, a coloring page, and Project WILD activities.

Hug a Tree and Other Things to do Outdoors with Young Children. R. Rockwell, E. Sherwood, and R. Williams. Mt. Rainier, MD: Gryphon House, Inc, 1986.

This activity book provides 40 experiences for young children to have with nature. Activities focus on aesthetic and affective experiences, observation experiences, data collecting, measurement experiences, and watching time and seasons. The authors provide information regarding ways to organize the outdoor experience and reference books for parents, teachers, and children.

I Need the Earth and the Earth Needs Me. (video) General Motors in cooperation with the U.S. EPA, 1990.

A live action video which shows children participating in conservation activities such as recycling, planting trees, and cleaning up rivers and lakeshores. The video is divided into mini-presentations on conserving or cleaning the air, land and water. A booklet enclosed with the video provides accompanying activities which are related to several curricular areas. Video length: 20 minutes. Grades 3-6.

Incorporating Environmental Education into the Primary School Curriculum. Faculty of Education, University of Malta, 1991.
Discusses the concepts, goals and objectives of environmental education, defines environmental education concepts, describes teaching methods, and provides sample activities and a glossary. The text is in English and Maltese.

The Interpreter's Guidebook. K. Regnier, M. Gross, R. Zimmerman. Steven's Point, WI: UW-SP Foundation Press, Inc., 1992.
A guide for naturalists interested in developing presentations and programs. Chapters include a) planning interpretive experiences, b) interpretive talks, c) slide talks, d) creative techniques, e) trail techniques, and f) interpretation for children. A resource section is also included.

Iowa Developed Energy Activity Sampler. Des Moines, IA: Iowa Department of Education: 1989.
Curriculum guide provides activities that utilize a learning cycle to develop a knowledgeable student population concerning energy matters. Decision making skills are emphasized and developing an energy conservation ethic is a major goal. Energy sources discussed in the guide include the sun, wind, water, electricity, fossil fuels and food. Grades K-5.

Investigating Nature through Outdoor Projects. V. Brown. Harrisburg, PA: Stackpole Books: 1983.
Provides 36 activities which incorporate scientific methods, such as observation and awareness, and the outdoors. Activities include adventures with mammals, birds, reptiles, insects and spiders, and different habitats.

Keepers of the Animals: Native American Stories and Wildlife Activities for Children. M. Caduto & J. Bruchac. Golden, CO: Fulcrum Publishing, 1991.
This book features a collection of North American Indian Stories and related hands-on activities designed to inspire children and promote responsible stewardship toward all animals. The emphasis is on an interdisciplinary approach to teaching about animals and Native American cultures. Student activities involve creative arts, theater, reading, writing, social studies, science and mathematics. Grades K-6.

Keepers of the Animals: Teacher's Guide. M. Caduto & J. Bruchac. Golden, CO: Fulcrum Publishing, 1992.
Describes in detail the information provided in *Keepers of the Animals*. The guide also provides supplementary text and reading lists keyed to the chapters of the Keepers. The chapters in the guide discuss ecological education, Native North American stories, the Native world of creation, and the formulation of the Native North American Environmental ethic.

Keepers of the Earth: Native American Stories and Environmental Activities for Children. M. Caduto & J. Bruchac. Golden, CO: Fulcrum, Inc., 1989.
This book features a collection of North American Indian Stories and related hands-on activities designed to inspire children and help them feel a part of their surroundings. The emphasis is on an interdisciplinary approach to teaching about the earth and Native American cultures. Student activities involve creative arts, theater, reading, writing, social studies, science and mathematics.

Kid's Gardening. L. Ocone, E. Pranis. : Burlington, VT: National Gardening Association, 1990.
Provides information regarding the planning, development and design of a garden for young people. Also provides activities and

basics of indoor and outdoor gardening.

The Kid's Nature Book. S. Milford. Charlotte, VT: Williamson Publishing, 1989.

An activity book written for children which provides a nature activity for every day of the year.

Let's Grow! 72 Gardening Activities with Children. L. Tilgner. Pownal, VT: Storey Communications, Inc, 1988.

Includes how to grow vegetables, flowers, herbs, etc., and how to plant, tend and harvest a garden. Introductory chapters address gardening with small children and with children with special needs, as well as how to get started with tools and garden preparation. Numerous projects follow, each complete with a list of tools and other items needed and time required. Projects range from toddlers to teenagers.

Living Lightly in the City. An Urban Environmental Education Curriculum Guide. M. O'Connor. Milwaukee, WI: Schlitz Audubon Center, 1990.

This curriculum guide is written for primary grade students in suburban and urban communities. The text is a compilation of ideas and materials to assist a teacher interested in incorporating environmental concepts into the existing curriculum.

The Lorax. (video) Dr. Seuss. New York: Playhouse Video, 1989.

The Lorax is a creature who speaks for the trees, trying to stop the profit-greedy Onceler from destroying the forest. A tale of progress run amok, the important warning is geared to the young, with an eye towards the world they will inherit tomorrow. Video length: 30 minutes.

Love the Earth: Exploring Environmental Activities for Young Children. P. Claycomb. Livonia, MI: Partner Press, Inc., 1991.

Offers both indoor and outdoor activiites that focus on similar concepts, such as insects, weather, animals, colors, and plants, plus a variety of related songs and fingerplays. Preschool.

Making the Right Connections: A Guide for Nature Writers. J. Heintzman. Stevens Point, WI: UW-SP Foundation Press, Inc., 1988.

A resource guide which describes how to write about the natural world in a way that is understandable to the reader.

Manure To Meadow To Milkshake. Jorgensen, Black & Hallesy. Los Altos Hills, CA.: Hidden Villa Environmental Education, 1991.

The Trust for Hidden Villa is meeting the challenges of the 90's by engaging children and adults in hands-on, innovative programs promoting environmental awareness and humanitarian values. This book provides the opportunity for hands-on experiences, to move from the experience to form concepts and then relate the experience to children's lives.

Marmalade Days (Fall, Winter, & Spring editions). C. Taylor-Bond. Livonia, MI: Partner Press, 1987.

Provides the preschool and kindergarten teacher with complete learning units. Included are activities for each subject, directions, ready made worksheets, patterns, and pictures of finished projects, words and actions of fingerplays and action songs, tunes or music for songs, recipes, and letters to parents.

Model Learner Outcomes for Environmental Education. St. Paul, MI: Minnesota Department of Education, 1991.

Part of the Environmental Education Curriculum Guide for the State of Minnesota. Describes the importance, contexts, and goals of environmental education. The model learner outcomes represent a set of possible end results of instruction. The outcomes are referenced to the cognitive, psychomotor, and affective domains. Outcomes that focus on multicultural, disability awareness, international, and gender fair concept development are also noted.

More Mudpies to Magnets. E. Sherwood, R. Williams, & R. Rockwell. Mt. Rainier, MD: Gryphon House, 1990.

    This curriculum guide includes 126 hands-on science experiments and activities. The instructions are clear and the results will hold the attention and excite the imagination of children ages 2-6. Science skills developed by the activities in the book include: classification, measuring, using space and time relationships, communication, predicting and inferring, and numbers. Each activity outlines new words, equipment required, procedural steps and enrichment ideas.

Mudpies to Magnets. E. Sherwood, R. Williams, & R. Rockwell. Mt. Rainier, MD: Gryphon House, 1987.

    This book presents a science curriculum based on the natural curiosity of children. Eight curriculum units contain 112 hands-on activities for ages 2-5. Each activity outlines new words, equipment required, procedural steps and enrichment ideas. Also includes tips on safety and planning and setting up a science activity center.

Mud, Sand, and Water. D. Hill. Washington, D.C.: Minnesota Department of Education, 1977.

    Describes how these materials can be used in early childhood classrooms to help children experience positive feelings and wonder and also offer opportunities for the beginning basis of science and math. Provides logistics for setting up a learning-living environment of mud, sand and water.

My Earth Book. L. Schwartz. Santa Barbara, CA: Learning Works, 1991.

    Contains pictures, puzzles, and projects created for children and written in simple language. Activities include coloring, follow the dots, mazes, dioramas and mobiles, and awards. The book covers littering, pollution, water conservation, endangered and other environmental topics.

My First Nature Book. A. Wilkes. New York: Alfred A. Knopf, 1990.

    A book written for children which provides indoor and outdoor nature activities. Simple and step-by-step instructions are given, as well as descriptions of the equipment needed and life size photographs of the finished projects. Activities include making a terrarium, bird feeder, caterpillar house, and worm farm.

My Recipes are for the Birds. I. Cosgrove. New York: Doubleday, 1976.

    Provides over 15 recipes for feeding different species of wild birds. Also describes how to set up bird feeding and nesting stations.

A Naturalist's Teaching Manual. J. Wilson. New York: Prentice Hall, 1986.

    A catalog of nature studies and activities which can be conducted indoors and out, day and night, summer or winter, rain or shine, and with individuals or groups. Over 100 projects and exercises which have been tested in state parks. Activities focus on awakening the senses, plants, birds, water and pond life, snow walks, and nature after dark.

Nature Activities for Early Childhood. J. Nickelsburg. Menlo Park, CA: Addison-Wesley Publishing Co., 1976.

    This book is designed to help teachers and parents provide young children with experiences in observing nature. It is planned to assist children to develop their senses, to sharpen their powers of observation, to improve their speech and to expand their aesthetic appreciation. The 44 projects include outdoor and indoor projects, projects with small animals, watching things, looking for things in the ground, and projects with plants.

Nature for the Very Young. M. Bowden. New York: John Wiley & Sons, 1989.

This handbook of activities offers a combination of preschool readiness material and learning activities that use nature exploration as a springboard for learning and growing. Lessons are built around background information for the adults and proven learning activities for the children. The material is designed to focus on the basic concepts appropriate to a young child's level of development and ability. These concepts include color recognition, sequencing, body awareness, and reading readiness. Readers will also find guidance on leading a group of young children on field trips. Ages 2-8.

Nature's Classroom: A Program Guide for Camps and Schools. Storer Camps. Martinsville, IN: American Camping Association, 1988.

An updated guide which assists instructors in planning outdoor experiences. The book represents over forty programming ideas, allowing instructors to create their own programs. The compilation includes basics for beginners as well as new ideas for the experienced. Chapters include Program Guide, Critters, Outdoor Feelings, Trees and Such, Back in Time, Challenge, The Good Earth, and Winter Watch.

Naturewatch: Exploring Nature with Your Children. A. Katz. Menlo Park, CA: Addison-Wesley Publishing Co., 1986.

Offers parents, teachers and children ways to explore and learn from the natural environment. Over 50 projects in the book require no special equipment or skills. With help from an adult, children will be able to tell the age of a tree or how to catch a spider's web intact. After learning to identify certain plants, children will be ready to create a garden of his or her own, indoors or outdoors. A section on nature crafts shows how to create treasures from materials found in nature.

Nature With Children of all Ages. E. Sisson. New York: Prentice Hall, 1982.

This illustrated handbook for outdoor learning with children provides ideas for rousing a child's curiosity, tips on managing groups in the outdoors, nature facts and information and instructions for projects using materials collected in nature. Each chapter covers either a group of living things, a season, or an environment. The emphasis is less on facts than on attitude and the sharpening of awareness.

Ocean Book, The. The Center for Marine Conservation. New York: John Wiley & Sons, Inc., 1989.

This activity book on the world of the oceans and the living things that inhabit them contains experiments, investigations, puzzles and games. The activities are designed to teach by doing; topics include whales, seals, sharks, camouflage, sea turtles, the ocean floor, and coral reefs. All the activities are ideal for grades K-6.

100 Teaching Activities in Environmental Education, Number One. J. Wheatley & H. Coon. Columbus, OH: ERIC Clearinghouse for Science, Mathematics, and Environmental Education, 1973.

This package contains activities in environmental education designed by students for use in grades K-12. Each activity has been classified by the editors according to the most appropriate grade level, subject matter, environmental concept involved, and environmental problem area. In addition to being classified by grade level, each activity contains a statement of purpose on how the activity may be used and a reference to a source where the activity may be found in more detail or with variations.

Open the Door, Let's Explore. R. Redleaf. Mt. Rainier, MD: Gryphon House, 1983.

This book contains ideas and activities associated with various field trips. Each trip lists several purposes one might consider for that trip, as well as vocabulary words that the children can learn as part of the experience. Included with each trip are original fingerplays and songs; selected books of fingerplays. Songs and general resource books are listed in an annotated bibliography. Preschool - kindergarten.

Outdoor Areas as Learning Laboratories. A. McCormack. Columbus, OH: ERIC Clearinghouse for Science, Mathematics, and Environmental Education, 1979.

This book is intended to be a source of ideas for outdoor learning activities appropriate for youngsters in elementary, middle and junior high schools. It may also be useful for anyone who works with children in outdoor settings. The first chapter presents a variety of approaches to using the outdoors for learning. Also, strategies for developing schoolyards as learning laboratories are suggested. The remainder of the book is a collection of activities good for outdoor settings. Chapters include animal studies, plant studies, ecology, physical science and interdisciplinary activities.

Outside Play and Learning Book, The. K. Miller. Mt. Rainier, MD: Gryphon House, 1989.

Hundreds of age-appropriate, challenging activities and games to engage the toddler or preschooler. A special chapter introduces infants to the outdoors. Other chapters include: Splish Splash: Things to Do With Water; Let it Snow! Let it Snow! Let it Snow!; and Dig it! Things to Do With Sand and Mud. Each activity includes ways of extending the play and what children learn from the play.

Plantworks. K. Shanberg and S. Tekiela. Cambridge, MN: Adventure Publications, 1991.

A guide book, cookbook and activity book in one. Provides over 50 recipes that include 15 common wild edible plants. The authors also provide the natural histories of the plants and over 20 nature activities.

Play and Playscapes. J. Frost. Albany, NY: Delmar Publishers, 1992.

This book deals with all aspects of child's play, child development, and play environment design, including play value and safety. Proceedings of major task forces to develop safety guidelines and standards are incorporated. Coverage includes implications for making play environments developmentally appropriate, and a special section on play environments for disabled children is provided.

Pond and Brook. M. Caduto. Englewood Cliffs, NJ: Prentice Hall, 1990.

Designed specifically for the amateur naturalist and filled with hands-on projects and activities, the book introduces readers to the world of freshwater life. All common freshwater environments, from wetlands and deep lakes, to streams and vernal ponds, are investigated. Readers will learn the unique properties of water, the basic principles vital to understanding aquatic life, and the origin of freshwater habitats.

Preschool/Primary Nature Kits. St. Paul, MN: Minnesota Department of Natural Resources.

An unbound collection of activity/coloring sheets which focus on animal and plant studies.

Program Planning Guide: Environmental Education. St. Paul, MN: Minnesota Department of Education, 1989.

This curriculum guide provides guidelines for environmental education objectives, methods for incorporating environmental education into existing curricula, planning suggestions for developing an environmental education program, and a bibliography of materials, resources and references.

Project WILD: Elementary. Boulder, CO: Western Regional Environmental Education Council, 1985.

Project WILD is an interdisciplinary, supplementary environmental and conservation education program emphasizing wildlife. Instructional activities within the Project WILD materials are designed for integration into school subject and skill areas. The activities are organized into seven major sections: a) awareness and appreciation, b) diversity of wildlife values, c) ecological principles, d) management and conservation, e) people, culture and wildlife, f) trends, issues, and consequences, and g) responsible human actions.

Rainbows, Mirages, and Sundogs: The Sky as a Source of Wonder. R. Gallant. New York: MacMillan Publishing Co., 1987.

The author shows beginners as well as more experienced sky watchers how to find, observe, and understand sky phenomena. Activities include taking trail star photographs, measuring sun halos, learning why stars twinkle, and finding a full circle rainbow.

Raising an Earth Friendly Child Level 1. D. Tilsworth. Fairbanks, AK: Raven Press, 1991.

An activity book divided into 52 chapters, with each chapter providing several activities to help children and their parents improve the environment. Each chapter includes background information, goals, age range, and materials needed.

Reaching for Connections (Vol. 1) Creative Ideas for Enhancing Educational and Interpretive Programs. D. Stokes. Milwaukee WI: Schlitz Audubon Center.

This activity book is meant to enhance educational and interpretive programs. The activities and material found in this book can be useful in teaching the following concepts: habitat and niche, territory, diversity and independence, competition and cooperation, and awareness and understanding. Each activity describes the grade/age level, number of people, energy level, procedure and conclusion.

Reaching for Connections (Vol. 2) Creative Exploration of Nature with Young Children. D. Stokes. Milwaukee, WI: Schlitz Audubon Center.

The activities in this guide book are designed to help parents and teachers build or reinforce positive connections between young children and Nature. The activities are direct, hands-on, and simple, beginning with the use of the five senses. Other foci include plants, songs, fingerplays and stories, the four seasons, and animals nobody loves. Ages 2-10.

Reflections. (video) Camden, Maine: Varied Directions, Inc.

Shows the Astronauts on Apollo IX, 1969, and one particular astronaut's recollection of his experiences while looking at the earth from space, and his feelings toward the earth and humanity. Video length: 16 minutes.

Save the Earth. B. Miles. New York: Alfred A. Knopf, 1991.

An environmental-action guide for children which includes factual information about the natural world, stories about children who have taken action in their communities, over 100 activities for kids to do themselves, and a how- to section that includes a resource list of environmental organizations and a full glossary and index.

Science Experiences for Preschoolers. L. Ukens. Columbus, OH: ERIC Clearinghouse for Science Mathematics and Environmental Education, 1986.

A collection of activities intended for use with children aged four and five. The intent of the activities is to get children involved in interacting with their environment. Through hands-on interaction with a variety of materials in a variety of ways, children start developing the idea that they can make a difference. The activities are divided into three areas: general activities, life science and the physical sciences. The sourcebook emphasizes inexpensive, easily obtained materials and equipment.

Science Experiences for the Early Childhood Years. J. Harlan. New York: Merril Publishing, 1988.

Describes a cognitive/affective approach to science instruction, emphasizing multi-modal activities. Also provides information to teachers regarding the introduction of science into the primary curriculum. Science concepts include plants, animals, weather and seasons, rocks and minerals, magnetism, and light. Appendices include references for music, records and poetry and salvage sources for science materials.

Science Through Children's Literature. C. Butzow & J. Butzow. Englewood, CO: Teacher's Ideas Press, 1989.

Provides an alternative approach to the teaching of elementary science through the selection of factually correct works of fictional children's literature. Part I of the book presents an integrated approach to scientific instruction using children's fictional literature as its foundation. The remainder of the book provides specific activities for teachers to use in the classroom, suggesting 33 children's books that can be adapted to the elementary curriculum. Parts II, III, and IV cover life science, earth and space science, and physical science, respectively.

Seahouse. (video) Chapel Hill, N.C: Environmental Media.

A video narrated by children which presents the diversity of life in the ocean. The tape is divided into ten five-minute programs which describe coral reefs, fish, camouflage, dangerous ocean animals, starfish, feeding habits, and the biology of fish. Video length: 50 minutes.

Sense of Wonder, The. R. Carson. Berkeley, CA.: Harper & Row Publishers, Inc., 1990.

Depicts the magic and beauty that is all about us in the natural world. The bright-colored photo essay accompanies and interprets Carson's words with great precision. Parents, Children and anyone who values natural beauty will treasure this reading experience.

Sharing Nature with Children. J. Cornell. Nevada City, CA: Dawn Publications, 1979.

Presents 42 activities which open up nature to children and adults. Each of the games creates a situation, or an experience, in which nature is the teacher. Each activity includes a reference chart which describes a) the basic mood of each game, b) the concepts, attitudes and qualities it teaches, c) when and where to play, d) number of players needed, e) best age range, and f) special materials needed. At the end of the book, the games are indexed in four ways: according to the attitudes and qualities they encourage in children; according to the qualities they teach; according to the environment in which they can best be used; and according to the mood they express.

Sharing the Joy of Nature. J. Cornell. Nevada City, CA: Dawn Publications, 1989.

This book is a sequel to *Sharing Nature with Children*, but activities can be used with children and adults. The author describes "Flow Learning", a method of leading nature activities which encourages people to awaken enthusiasm, focus attention, relate a direct experience, and share inspiration. Each activity includes a reference chart similar to the one mentioned in *Sharing Nature with Children*.

Sharing the Joy of Nature. (video) J. Cornell. Nevada City, CA: Dawn Publications, 1991.

In this video, Joseph Cornell demonstrates the four basic types of nature activities and how they can be used to increase children's and adult's awareness and empathy for the natural world. Activities include "Build a Tree," "Sounds," "Animals, Animals," "Camera Game," "Bird Calling," "Tree Imagery," and "Nature Meditations." These activities can also be found in *Sharing the Joy of Nature* and *Sharing Nature with Children*. Video length: 40 minutes.

Signs of Fall: A Fall Activity Packet for Pre-School. M. Monroe, Jackson, MI: Dahlem Environmental Education Center of the Jackson Community College, 1982.

This activity packet identifies goals and objectives for fall activities. The packet also includes many pre-trip activities, a field trip and post-trip activities plus references.

Signs of Spring: A Spring Activity Packet for Pre-School. M. Monroe, Jackson, MI: Dahlem Environmental Education Center of the Jackson Community College, 1984.

This activity packet identifies goals and objectives for spring activities. The packet also includes many pre-trip activities, a field trip and post-trip activities plus references.

Signs, Trails, and Wayside Exhibits. S. Trapp, M. Gross, and R. Zimmerman. Stevens Point, WI: UW-SP Foundation Press, Inc.

Handbook describes how to create signs, trails, and exhibits for use in recreational nature areas.

Spin, Spider, Spin. Songs for a Greater Appreciation of Nature. (record album) P. Zeitlin. Freeport, NY: Educational Activities, Inc., 1974.

Ten animal songs and lyrics are included on this album.

Starting Small in the Wilderness: The Sierra Club Outdoors Guide for Families. M. Doan. San Francisco, CA: Sierra Club Books, 1979.

A parent's guide to backcountry adventure with children, covering a wide range of family camping activities for all seasons. The author emphasizes the special responsibilities involved in sharing the wilderness experience with children: providing games and amusements during inclement weather, establishing camp rules, teaching safety and first aid, as well as the joys of discovering the natural world. The author also reviews the gear necessary for wilderness travel, including clothing and equipment difficult to obtain for children.

Students Working Against Trash: Guide to School Beautification. Cleveland, OH: Clean-Land, Ohio, 1989.

This instructional manual provides educational reinforcement for skills currently taught at the 4th, 5th, and 6th grade levels. The manual includes sections related to different subject areas: math, reading, environmental science, social studies, health, family life and safety education. An environmental attitude survey and bibliography are also included. The guide to school beautification was created to assist teachers, principals, and other educators with the implementation of small scale landscaping and beautification projects on school grounds with their students. Step-by-step information is provided on planning the project, raising funds, selecting plant materials, planting, and ongoing care.

Super Saver Investigators. Columbus, OH: Ohio Department of Natural Resources, 1990.

The activities in this guidebook provide opportunities for students to investigate the environmental impacts of the generation of waste in our society and to investigate solutions to the waste crisis. The activities cross disciplines to link subjects of science, social studies and language arts, often including exercises related to arts and crafts, drama and music. Fifteen chapters in the guide include background information, specific activities, objectives, methods, preparation, vocabulary words, handouts, procedures and evaluation. Grades K-6.

Talking to Fireflies, Shrinking the Moon. E. Duensing. New York: Penguin Books, 1990.

This guide to safe, environmentally sound outdoor activities for children and adults shares the facts and fun that were once part of America's rural heritage. The activities are categorized as warm or cold weather, or year round activities.

Teaching Activities in Environmental Education, (Volumes 2&3). J. Wheatley & H. Coon. Columbus, OH: ERIC Clearinghouse for Science, Mathematics, and Environmental Education, 1974, 1975.

These publications are designed for student use in grade K through 12. Each activity has been classified by the editors according to the most appropriate grade level, subject matter (science, mathematics, social studies, language arts, and fine arts), environmental concept involved, and environmental problem area. Each activity contains 1) a statement of purpose on how the activity may be used, and 2) a reference to a source where the activity may be found with more detail or with variations.

Teaching Kids to Love the Earth. M. Herman, J. Passineau, A. Schimpf, P. Treuer. Duluth, MN: Pfeifer-Hamilton Publishers, 1991.

A collection of 186 activities designed for use with children of all ages to help them experience and appreciate the earth. Each chapter contains a story, instructions for a main activity, suggestions for related activities, and a list of additional resources.

There Lived a Wicked Dragon. M. Finan. Washington, D.C.: U.S. Environmental Protection Agency, 1973.

A coloring book for children which tells the story of a dragon who feeds on litter and pollution, but is stopped when people in communities begin to recycle, commute, and respect the natural world.

Thinking Globally and Acting Locally: Environmental Education Teaching Activities. L. Mann & W. Stapp. Columbus, OH: ERIC Clearinghouse for Science, Mathematics, and Environmental Education, 1982.

The activities in this volume stress similarities between cultures rather than differences, provide clear pictures of the interconnectedness of systems and people, and the relationships between nations. The activities are also constructed to motivate action; in virtually every case, a step is included to involve learners in examining how their own behavior impacts people and/or the environment in other parts of the world. Instructional topics include: food production and distribution, energy, transportation, solid waste, pollution, population, endangered species, and life-style and environment. Grades K-12.

This Planet is Mine. M. Metzger & C. Whittaker. New York: Fireside/ Simon & Schuster, 1991.

This guide for parents and teachers describes and explains environmental issues, describes how to adapt your explanation to children of different ages, offers ways adults and family members can help, and presents many learning activities for the home or classroom. The book makes the environmental topic relevant and the participation hands-on. Projects include adopting a whale, creating a mini-tropical rain forest, making raisins, growing a worm farm, and making recycled paper.

Trends and Issues Related to the Preparation of Teachers for Environmental Education. J. Disinger & R. Howe. Columbus, OH: ERIC Clearinghouse for Science, Mathematics, and Environmental Education, 1990.

Reviews the literature pertaining to teacher education in, about, and for environmental education. The recent and current status of environmental education in United States elementary and secondary schools is discussed, as well as the implications for teacher education, the foundation and content competencies for environmental educators, current teacher activities in the field, and trends and issues in pre-service and inservice teacher education for environmental learning.

Water Magic. M. Haberman. Denver, CO: American Water Works Association, 1991.

This book describes 23 hands-on activities in which each lesson identifies a specific objective, the curriculum area (such as social studies or art), and cognitive taxonomy. Every curriculum area used in the lower primary grades is covered by at least one activity in this book. Two tables are included which allow educators to find which activities address specific areas of the curriculum and to give an overview of the intellectual processes addressed by specific activities. A glossary of water-related terms is also included, as well as a bibliography of water-related resource books for educators. Grades K-3.

Water, Stones, and Fossil Bones. K. Lind (editor). Washington, DC: National Science Teacher's Association, 1991.

These 51 hands-on activities, teacher-written and teacher-tested, will help encourage students' natural curiosity. Cut a riverbed, cook hot dogs on a solar cooker, make fog, measure raindrops, filter water, and more, all with easily obtainable materials. Each activity includes background information to introduce the activity, a description of concepts and skills to be developed, step-by-step procedures, questions keyed to the procedure to help you guide student discussion and probe understanding, and suggestions for further investigations. Grades K-8.

Natural Beginnings Teacher Training Guide

Natural Beginnings, a teacher training guide based on Fostering a Sense of Wonder During the Early Childhood Years, is scheduled to be available in the Fall of 1995. This training guide, outlining a four-day workshop focusing on environmental education at the early childhood level, is designed to prepare preschool teachers to infuse environmental education into all aspects of their curriculum. Qualifications to lead this workshop include a strong background in early childhood education, an understanding of the rationale and guidelines for environmental education at the early childhood level, and a familiarity with the principles and practices outlined in Fostering a Sense of Wonder During the Early Childhood Years. While an early childhood education curriculum specialist might serve as the leader of the proposed workshop, it is highly recommended that both an environmental education professional and a teacher educator also be involved in the implementation of the workshop. Guidelines and suggestions for how this might be arranged are outlined in the training guide. Individuals interested in this publication should refer to it as the Natural Beginnings Teacher Training Guide.

Natural Beginnings Resource Book

Another publication relating to environmental education at the early childhood level will be available in Spring, 1996. This publication will consist of a compilation of selected environmental education units and descriptions of related activity kits developed by the preschool teachers participating in the Natural Beginnings workshop offered at Bowling Green State University in Summer, 1995. Individuals interested in this publication should refer to it as the Natural Beginnings Resource Book.